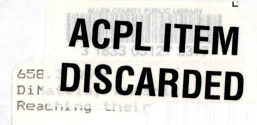

A TI

REACHING THEIR MINDS

A Trainer's Manual for Rational Effectiveness Training

by Dominic DiMattia, Ed.D.
and Drs. Theo IJzermans

INSTITUTE FOR RATIONAL-EMOTIVE THERAPY
New York

Published by
The Institute for Rational-Emotive Therapy
45 East 65th Street, New York, NY 10021

PRINTED IN THE UNITED STATES OF AMERICA

Library of Congress Catalog Number: 95-82381

ISBN 0-917476-25-5

Table of Contents

Foreword

Rational Effectiveness Training first evolved in 1967, when I and Dr. Milton L. Blum, head of the Industrial/ Organization Department of the Baruch School of Business of the City College of New York, published our first paper on it in *Psychological Reports.* Dr. Blum had read several of my early papers on rational-emotive psychology and realized that this form of counseling was ideally suited for people working in business and industry

This paper, "Rational Training: A New Method of Facilitating Management and Labor Relations," was later expanded into my book, *Executive Leadership: A Rational Approach.* Also, in cooperation with Dr. Leonard Haber of Miami, I began giving a series of talks and workshops for managers and executives and my associates and I have continued to do so ever since.

For the past decade, Dr. Dominic DiMattia has been the main presenter of Rational Effectiveness Training (RET) in the United States, the Netherlands, and Australia and has given more corporate workshops and talks, as our Director of Corporate Services and as Associate Executive Director of our Institute, than any other person. Several years ago he was joined by Drs. Theo IJzermans of Amsterdam, a psychologist and corporate trainer with Schouten and Nelissen, a major training and management consulting organization in The Netherlands.

The present book brings Rational Effectiveness Training up to date. It clearly and effectively shows how it can be used in sales, management, organizational development, and many other important aspects of business and industry. It explains the main irrational beliefs that business people often have, how they can zero in on them and change them, and how they can help themselves and their organizations, as well as improve their personal and social lives. It presents several of the main techniques of Rational Effectiveness Training, including active disputing of irrational beliefs, rational emotive imagery, and homework assignments. It includes a number of interesting and useful case presentations. It shows readers how to tackle the two biggest emotional problems that plague them at work and at play—their feelings of inadequacy and their low frustration tolerance.

People are highly complicated; and clearly no book is going to show them how to function entirely effectively in all aspects of their lives. But this book packs so much common sense and forceful self-help suggestions into a brief space that it will enable attentive and hardworking readers to get off to a fine personal and work-related start. Happy and productive reading!

Albert Ellis, Ph.D., *President*
Institute for Rational-Emotive Therapy
New York City

CHAPTER 1

Introduction to Rational Effectiveness Training

Today, people strive for work that is intrinsically rewarding and meaningful and allows them:

- to grow;
- to develop meaningful relationships;
- to be creative; and
- to balance their lives.

It is vital that today's workers have the interpersonal skills to lead them through teamwork and problem-solving without biased judgment or emotional interference.

Rational Effectiveness Training provides a clear, easy-to-understand model for interpersonal communication and emotional self-management. It teaches people to work as team members so that they may solve problems in a cooperative manner by remaining flexible and open. It helps individuals to identify the causes of their emotional reactions and learn to change the ideas and beliefs that may result in conflict and stress.

Rational training focuses on providing a personal growth experience that leads to self-improvement in the workplace. It specifically shows people how to eliminate fears of failure, become more tolerant and less hostile, gain improved self-acceptance, and tolerate situations that are frustrating. Thus, a more stable and productive environment is created through reducing hostile and angry attitudes.

Specific skills in the following areas will help you attain self-improvement and, in turn, organizational improvement. You will learn to:

- Become more tolerant and less hostile toward superiors, associates, and subordinates;

- Gain unqualified self-acceptance and self-respect;

- Reduce anxiety and insecurity;

- Gain maximum self-determination;

- Achieve high frustration tolerance.

An Example of How Rational Effectiveness Training Works

Lauren, a sales associate at Waterford Software Company, has been thinking lately about jumping ship. Her sales figures and commissions have been falling off and it is her opinion that Waterford has not remained competitive in its product development. Due to recent cutbacks, which had been necessary in a soft market, Waterford has not been putting money into Research and Development. As Lauren confided, "How can you stay competitive in this field when you're not putting out state-of-the-art software?"

In fact, Lauren has not been seeing as many clients per week as she had six months ago. "It's just not fair," she tells herself. "Why do I have to work so hard to sell these low-tech products? I'm embarrassed to have my name associated with this company. What must people think of me as I face my customers and claim to believe in the quality of the software we sell?"

Enter Rational Effectiveness Training

Members of Lauren's Rational Effectiveness group discuss Lauren's problem situation. The attitudes and beliefs that are driving Lauren's discomfort become the focus of the training and development activity. By examining examples of the types of situations that are likely to arise on the job, the group member experiences his or her positive and negative reactions to various work conflicts. Further, the member determines what *practical* steps might be taken to solve the problem. By focusing on cognitive, behavioral, and experiential methods, participants are substantially helped to decrease their irrational and self-defeating attitudes.

First espoused by psychologist Albert Ellis in 1955, RET relies on a simple A-B-C approach. *A* is the Activating event, *B* is the set of Beliefs and attitudes that influence behavior, and *C* are the resulting feelings and behavior, or Consequences.

In Lauren's case, the Activating event (*A*) is the cutback in Research and Development. The Consequence (*C*) was her becoming highly frustrated and giving up. But *A* didn't cause *C*. Rather, it is *B*, Lauren's beliefs and attitudes about the corporate decision to shut down Research and Development, that caused *C*.

RET teaches the participants to replace perfectionistic and frustration-producing thinking with positive and rational ideas that enhance productivity. Now, back to Lauren.

In class, Lauren was taught how to practice positive self-talk. By learning to dispute her *disabling* thoughts, she can then replace them with more rational and *motivating* ones. Her belief that "It's not fair" is replaced by "Who ever said we live in a fair world? I can change jobs, but there are no guarantees that the situation will be better elsewhere."

Her thought "Why do I have to work so hard?" becomes replaced by the self-message that "If I can sell in these slow times, I can work on improving my selling skills and be able to sell anything, anytime. Besides, Waterford is a good solid company, and with people like me on its team, sales will pick up and we'll be able to put more money into Research and Development again."

"I'm embarrassed to have my name associated with this company" and "What must people think of me?" become changed to "There will always be people who scoff at others, but that doesn't have to stop me from doing what I know to be right. As long as I believe in myself and these products—which, while not new, have withstood the test of time—I'll be able to sell them."

Since emotional self-management training is, to a large extent, self-help oriented, the skills and strategies that workshop participants learn are designed to be readily applied in the work setting.

Many organizations emphasize the need for employees to do an excellent job and often punish employees who make mistakes. Therefore, when the RET concept of accepting *yourself* as fallible is introduced, there may be serious resistance because it is misinterpreted as meaning accepting inadequate *performance.*

Richard, a manager with a Fortune 500 high tech company, was suddenly stymied when his company began its new Campaign for Excellence. He'd done excellent work before, but he was terrorized by the dramatized need for Excellence with a capital *E*. He began procrastinating on putting together presentations to the point where his superiors took note of his sudden change in style. After an RET intervention, where he learned to dispute the irrational belief that it would be terrible if he did anything less than perfect, he was freed to begin working again.

RET will actually help improve performance, since the anxiety and tension created by perfectionistic thinking are reduced and employees can then focus on completing tasks rather than avoiding them. RET helps people achieve excellence with a minimum of distress. It is *not* an approach which lowers standards; instead, it focuses on a different strategy to *achieve high standards*.

Meeting deadlines is another example. "I *must* complete this task on time" becomes a self-defeating thought when it results in extreme anxiety and tension that actually interfere with getting the job done. Worrying about a task doesn't get it completed more quickly; it only distracts you from focusing on it effectively. RET acknowledges the importance of meeting deadlines, but teaches that *obsessing* about them is counter-productive. RET provides strategies for achieving organizational goals which reduce counter-productive behavior.

Today's workers are mobile, often switching companies five or six times within their career. As in Lauren's case, this may be because the employee is responding to a poor work environment. Instead of developing a framework of beliefs that can help her or him adjust to the corporate world, the employee leaves. These rigid demands that the workplace *must* be trouble-free and provide perfect job satisfaction *without any discomfort*, are irrational and unrealistic.

The same employee may leave an organization if career

advancement is not happening fast enough or if she is not promoted to the exact position needed for advancement. Such perfectionistic demands result in employees leaving to find the perfect work environment, only to encounter the same or other roadblocks in their next job.

There is no end to this cycle: since perfection is not attainable in a fallible world, the employee never finds the perfect job in the perfect city for the perfect salary. And organizations pay the price through turnover, absenteeism, poor morale, and lack of employee commitment.

CHAPTER 2

Changing Cognitions and Learning New Behavior

No matter how well organized or presented a training program is, we cannot control the ability of the participants to learn and accept the material. As trainers, we are constantly frustrated by participants who seem unable or unwilling to embrace the material.

It is important to understand the relationship between learning and cognition (thinking) in order to facilitate the learning process. Participants come to training programs with certain mind sets. These mind sets are made up of beliefs and ideas which can either facilitate their learning or hinder it.

Let's take John, for example, a first line manager who was recently promoted to a managerial position. He was a very conscientious employee who was always on time and responded to authority unquestioningly. He was also very thorough and rarely made mistakes. To help him in his new position, he has been sent to a seminar on Communication Skills. Although he listens to the leader and takes notes during the lectures, when it comes to the role-playing exercises, he often gets frustrated and annoyed when the other person does not quickly respond to his requests. He incorporates in his communication the techniques suggested by the leader, but quickly gives up and begins questioning the usefulness of these techniques.

What keeps John from effectively using these techniques? It is obvious that John has a certain set of ideas or beliefs about the way others *should* respond to his communication. He strongly believes that employees should always defer to their bosses. This idea or cognition creates frustration and sometimes anger when employees do not react as he believes they should. When he is in this agitated state, John is unable to learn and maintain new behavior and falls back on old habits of demanding or commanding. His communication training is thus hindered. This is just one example of how rigid beliefs can interfere with learning during a training workshop.

One common belief which participants often come to workshops with is "I must always do very well and if I don't, I'm a failure." Individuals who attend training seminars often view themselves as successful and it is very important to them to maintain this view. Frequently they are highly perfectionistic and cannot tolerate any errors or mistakes in their performance. These perfectionistic ideas make it very difficult for them to learn new material, especially when it involves complex human behavior. It is easy for these perfectionists to study material and master it, but when asked to change long-time behavior patterns, the change is slow; and when they experience difficulty in mastering the new skills, they often become defensive and hostile. This then further prevents them from learning the skills.

A Case of Perfectionism

Mary is a highly successful financial analyst who has progressed rapidly in her company. She is one of the few women who work in her office and she views herself as succeeding because she rarely makes mistakes and puts in loads of extra hours to demonstrate that she is equal to any of the men in the office. She believes any errors would threaten her position.

Mary is currently attending a management training workshop which emphasizes cooperative decision-making with subordinates. It requires that she conduct a simulated meeting, during which the group is to arrive at a decision which is acceptable to everyone. Mary has been very attentive during the lectures and is sincere in trying to incorporate the ideas presented. However, when she conducted the problem-solving session, several members of the group were not cooperating and would not compromise. Mary immediately began to think the leaders would view her as incompetent if her group did not arrive at a decision. These cognitions made her very anxious and she became very authoritarian, which resulted in further resistance from group members. She then became defensive and began rejecting the ideas presented by the trainer.

If Mary were not so perfectionistic and did not place so much emphasis on succeeding, she might have learned from the experience and received useful feedback from the leader and other workshop participants. With practice she might have learned how to successfully run a meeting and handle resistance in a group. Her idea that she "must not fail" made it exceptionally difficult for her to learn new skills.

When we are thinking rationally it is easy for us to understand how unrealistic it is to think that we *should* be able to perform complex tasks well when we have never done them before. We do not learn to play the piano or master a sport without years of practice and many, many mistakes. Our demand that we not make mistakes, i.e., our perfectionism, keeps us from trying new behaviors. Trainers often see these cognitions interfering with learning during workshops.

Low Frustration Tolerance

Another cognitive constraint which can interfere with learning during a workshop is *low frustration tolerance*. Many participants demand that they see relevance immediately and not be be bored by uninteresting material. Often learning requires that we focus on information that is not necessarily interesting, in order to learn to function effectively. Also, before we can learn new tasks we may often have to engage in repetitive behaviors which may be tedious. When people insist that every subject be interesting and easy, they often become frustrated before they master the skill and gain reinforcement from mastery. People who are able to tell themselves that "even though this is difficult or boring I can still tolerate it—it will be worth the effort in the long run" often reduce their frustration and more efficiently master the skills being taught.

The combination of perfectionism *and* low frustration tolerance can significantly interfere with group participants' ability to learn. As trainers we need to be aware of these cognitions and assist trainees in our workshops by teaching them how to restructure their demanding *shoulds* into *preferences*.

It is also important to recognize how rigid beliefs affect creativity and initiating behavior. Many of us believe that creativity is a genetic characteristic which some lucky people have inherited. However, there is an alternative way to view creativity: creativity is the result of flexible and adaptable thinking. When we are free of any preconceived ideas about a solution to a problem we are often better able to explore more alternatives. Thus, we expand our repertoire of responses.

Often people are taught that there is one "right" way to manage or complete a task. We spend too much time in education teaching people to conduct themselves according to a particular approach; and once they are employed we also insist that policies and procedures must be rigidly adhered to. This type of black-and-white thinking often limits people's creativity. When confronted with a problem they simply rely on their beliefs and ideas on how to solve it and often ignore several variables which might change the dynamics of a situation.

For instance, even while the workforce is changing dramatically, managers tend to try to motivate employees by using the same old techniques that worked in the past. When confronted with failure, they often become frustrated and give up. This is because they are thinking "Employees should respond to my approach," rather than viewing this as a problem to solve and generating possible alternative solutions. When we are locked into one particular solution to a problem, our creativity is restricted. When we have rigid or unbending ideas about the way things "should" be done, we remain limited in our ability to develop creative solutions to our problems.

Many businesses are currently facing a rapidly changing world economy which is very competitive. The businesses that have managers with flexible ideas will come up with solutions to the new world conditions; those businesses that continue to think that they should operate in the same old ways will not come up with creative solutions. Let's bring this concept to a more personal level.

A manager is confronted with the development of a new marketing plan for his office. As he sits down to brainstorm new ideas, he continues to fall back on the typical approach of developing a brochure and conducting follow-up calls. He holds a meeting with his staff, and each time a new idea is presented he claims that it won't work or is "inappropriate." He is restricted by his rigid beliefs about how things should be marketed; as a result, no new ideas can emerge. Only when he learns to free himself from his preconceived ideas will his creativity emerge. "Shoulds" or "should nots" about anything will preclude creativity, since creativity is usually the development of *untried* ideas.

CHAPTER 3

Common Popular Irrational Beliefs

Perfectionism

Dan is one of the plant managers of an international electronics company. He is successful, ambitious, and a potential candidate for a directorship. He works 12 hour days, and spends at least half the weekend at the office. His wife, Diane, is a fundraiser for a not-for-profit organization.

Dan expects an offer to become a general plant manager in another factory 600 miles away. It is the next logical step in his career en route to a position at Corporate headquarters. But Diane and Leah, their 15-year-old daughters, refuse to move to another city. "You will spend most of your time at work," they argue, "but we will have to start all over again."

Dan is a perfectionist whose slogan in life is "Every mistake is one too many." As a result, he is a poor delegator. While he is working late and weekends, his staff is left feeling bored and under-utilized.

Highly sensitive to critical remarks from his superiors, Dan becomes extremely anxious during and after board meetings if his production line is met with criticism. At times, his anxiety blocks him so much that he is unable to think of solutions to the problem at hand; and he often blows up at the slightest critical remark.

Dan's case illustrates some of the problems a perfectionistic manager can create. He spends too much time on his job because of an inability to delegate, which impinges on his personal life. Criticism causes him intense anxiety, which hinders his creativity.

This unhealthy perfectionism, according to RET theory, is caused by an irrational belief system that says, "If I make a mistake, I am a failure as a *person*." The person equates every mistake as a measurement of his own worth, instead of recognizing his fallibility as a normal human being.

Dan's case shows how rigid and destructive perfectionism can lead to personal stress and interpersonal conflicts and inhibit creative problem-solving. Although perfectionism and "excellence" may be a part of the corporate culture, they can also block risk-taking and the acceptance of mistakes, which is part of a successful entrepreneurial spirit.

The Need to Be Loved

Sheila is the head of sales for a restaurant equipment import company. She is considered a warm and understanding manager, and her subordinates often invite her to their children's weddings and other social affairs.

Lately, sales figures have been way down. Sheila has tried motivational "pep talks" with her team, but they haven't helped. Last year, team members were all given satisfactory performance appraisals based on their promises to improve.

But now that the company is losing money, Sheila knows she will have to let some of her team go if their performance doesn't improve. Terrified of conflict and confrontation, she believes "I can only motivate my staff if they *like* me." Her continuing fear of being rejected by her subordinates prevents her from giving constructive feedback and thus undermines her effectiveness as a manager.

"I Shouldn't Have to Do Such Boring Work"

William is a hard-working staff member at a chemical company. Every staff member is required to fill out forms on the time allotted to different tasks. This takes about an hour a week, but William hates doing it and postpones it until it reaches monumental proportions. He often thinks about it on his drive home and resolves, "I'll do it tomorrow"— only to put it off again and again. His procrastination is caused by the underlying philosophy that "I shouldn't have to do such boring work. Work should be interesting and inspiring."

Demanding that work (and life in general) be easy and interesting is an ideology that leads to low frustration tolerance, or LFT.

"People Should Perform the Way I Expect Them to"

Pia is a newly hired manager at a pharmaceutical company. Her subordinates have been so fearful of her aggressive outbursts when she discovers their mistakes, that they have taken to hiding much of their work from her—when they do it at all.

Her entire department is hindered by Pia's philosophy that "People should be blamed for their mistakes. They must always perform as I expect them to; their work should be as perfect as mine." In reality, while it is the job of the manager to teach employees to perform to her expectations, she would better also allow them creative freedom for their own unique contribution—in which case, some mistakes are inevitable.

These examples show how companies divert a great deal of energy into ineffective conflicts, caused by the irrational demands people make on themselves and others. The most popular irrational demands are: "I should be perfect," "Everybody must like me," and "Life should be easy and interesting and without significant hassles."

Observation of everyday events shows a different reality. Mistakes *are* made; managers become unpopular when they request difficult and nasty tasks people don't like; and yes, some tasks are boring, difficult or extremely frustrating.

Another irrational aspect of these absolutistic ideas is their dysfunctionality: *they don't help the workers reach their goals.* Demanding perfection of oneself causes anxiety, which then leads to *more* mistakes. Demanding that people like you leads to the absence of a consistent vision, which subordinates find confusing. Demanding obedience leads to resistance. Low frustration tolerance leads to procrastination and in the long run, more energy gets spent avoiding tasks than actually doing them.

The above are examples of individuals' irrational beliefs. But often these beliefs are part of the corporate culture: "Our people should be perfect," "Managers should be well-liked by their subordinates," "All employees must always do what they are told," and "If they are the right people for the job, they will find the work interesting and enjoyable."

Organizational problems that result from these belief systems include avoidance of risk-taking and creativity—two essential ingredients for growth.

CHAPTER 4

Rational Effectiveness Training: Background and Theory

Traditionally, behavior change models have been dominated by three major schools of thought concerning the nature and treatment of emotional disturbance. These include classical psychoanalysis, behavior therapy and neuropsychiatry. Although markedly different in their interpretations of human behavior, these approaches have one similarity: their neglect of people's *conscious* ideas and thoughts as significant factors in determining their behavior.

Classical psychoanalysis considers conscious thoughts as simply representations of unconscious conflicts that are actually causing the disturbance. Behavior therapists until recently have disregarded the importance of thinking in their determination to assert themselves as the only true "scientists" among the different schools: since only overt, observable behavior can be measured, thoughts and ideas are rejected as invalid data. Finally, traditional neuropsychiatry has reduced conscious thought to simply a manifestation of underlying physical processes or clues to a disturbance in neurochemistry.

In recent years, an increasing number of writers has begun to emphasize the importance of conscious ideation in the treatment of emotional disturbance. Approaches which emphasize cognitive psychology are growing in number and are commonly referred to as "cognitive-behavioral." Included among them are Rational Emotive Behavior Therapy (Ellis, 1958, 1962), Cognitive Therapy (Beck, 1976), Rational Behavior Therapy (Maultsby, 1975), Interpersonal Cognitive Problem-Solving (Spivack, Platt and Shure, 1976), Cognitive Behavior Modification (Meichenbaum, 1977; Mahoney, 1974) and Multimodal Behavior Therapy (Lazarus, 1976). A review of the cognitive behavioral approaches is included to show how Rational Effectiveness Training can be especially effective in the work setting.

Rational Emotive Behavior Therapy

Albert Ellis originated rational-emotive therapy (now known as REBT or rational emotive behavior therapy) in 1955, and for years it stood almost alone as an active-directive form of therapy which placed cognition as the most important determinant of human emotion. Ellis has continued to expand and refine his therapeutic approaches to the point where REBT is today an internationally recognized therapy and is a leader among a growing number of cognitive-behavioral approaches.

Rational Effectiveness Training is largely based on rational emotive behavior therapy. It has not only contributed significantly to our understanding of emotional disturbance and its treatment, but has also become a major force in educating the general public in preventive approaches to mental health. It has become a multifaceted form of therapy that utilizes a wide variety of cognitive and behavioral methods and a large number of emotive-evocative-expressive methods such as role-playing, unconditional acceptance of the client, self-disclosure, and shame-attacking exercises.

Although REBT's concept of human personality includes the factors of biological predisposition and cultural influence, it places currently-held cognition at the core of human functioning. *We are ultimately responsible for how we feel by what we choose to believe or not believe.* We are born into this world with certain mental and physical characteristics and are strongly influenced by our families and friends, but how we feel is ultimately a function of how we *perceive* and evaluate these events over which we may not have had any control. So in the final analysis, we are currently responsible for how we feel and how seriously disturbed we make ourselves.

However, it should be made clear that Ellis does not view all neurotic problems as stemming only from irrational thinking. Human functioning is a result of cognitive *and* emotive *and* behavioral factors—all working together. As he stated in the original edition of *A Guide to Rational Living,*

> *We function, then, as a single organism—perceiving, moving, thinking and emoting simultaneously and interrelatedly. These four basic life processes are not distinctly different ones, each of which begins where the others leave off. Instead, they all significantly overlap and are in some respects aspects of the same thing.*

REBT hypothesizes that we are raised in a society that perpetuates irrational ideas and we keep reindoctrinating ourselves over and over with these beliefs until we come to view them as facts. These irrational beliefs can be categorized into three major demands:

(1) *Demands for acceptance and approval.* Examples of this demand are the commonly accepted ideas that "I must be loved and accepted by virtually all significant people in my environment" and "It is impossible for me to be happy if I

don't consistently have their approval."

(2) *Demands for competence.* An example of this is the belief that "I must be successful at every endeavor I choose to engage in, and if I fail I have no worth; I only have worth as long as I am achieving."

(3) *Demands for justice.* The beliefs that "the world should be fair and others should treat me differently" usually fall into this category. REBT posits that these types of absolutistic thinking create most of our emotional disturbance; and only if we begin to accept a more realistic view of people and the world will we become free from our debilitating emotions.

These concepts are often summarized in what is called the "A-B-C Theory of Emotional Disturbance." *A* is the Activating event, or the happening in our life which we often see as the cause for our unhappiness. *C* is the emotional Consequences, such as anxiety, depression, or anger. Most people think that *A* causes *C*; according to REBT, however, *C* is not a direct result of *A* but also a result of *B* — our Belief system or attitude *about* the event. When we upset ourselves about the event it is a result of an irrational *must* or *should* we are thinking about the event. For example, if you are fired from your job (A) and you have fallen into a depression (C), it is not losing the job that caused your depression, but rather your demand (at B) that it *should* not have happened and because it happened you are no good. It is the constant repetition of this thought that depresses you; and any change in your emotional state will result only if those irrational thoughts and beliefs are changed. In counseling this is commonly done by teaching the client to dispute (D) these irrational thoughts and replace them with more realistic and productive beliefs.

REBT is essentially an active-directive approach to therapy. The therapist is viewed as a teacher whose primary role is to counsel clients in (1) becoming aware of their irrational or illogical thoughts and (2) challenging or disputing their disturbing thoughts so they can replace them with more logical and efficient processes. The REBT counselor participates actively rather than merely being a passive listener. This process is not to be interpreted as lecturing or moralizing to the clients, but rather as questioning and analyzing in order to help clients better to understand and change their illogical thinking. In achieving these goals considerable latitude is available for individual therapist style. Actually, any method or technique which will assist clients to look at, question and change their irrational beliefs is consistent with rational emotive behavior therapy.

To strengthen and generalize the work that is done during the session, homework is often assigned to clients so that they can practice their new learnings and desensitize themselves to anxiety provoking situations. When they are assigned behavioral tasks, they are armed with accompanying cognitive strategies to prevent their emotional reactions from interfering with their completing the tasks.

Other strategies used by REBT therapists include rational emotive imagery, systematic desensitization, positive reinforcement, assertiveness training, modeling, bibliotherapy, role-playing, shame-attacking exercises, hypnotherapy and a wide range of other behavioral and emotive-expressive techniques. REBT therapists do not restrict themselves to disputing irrational beliefs, but use other methods which can help clients change the beliefs and assumptions that are driving their emotional disturbances.

Therefore, rational emotive behavior therapy assumes that although some biological and social forces strongly lead to irrationality, people have the potential for being rational. Emotional disturbances are largely caused by irrational thinking and can be remedied by changing such thinking. Therefore, a major goal of counseling and psychotherapy is to teach clients to think rationally.

Cognitive Therapy

Cognitive therapy, as developed by Aaron Beck (1976), differs in emphasis from Ellis' rational emotive behavior therapy. Although both cognitive therapy and REBT recognize that thoughts are the major determinants of human behavior, Beck considers "faulty learnings"—rather than irrational beliefs—as the cause of emotional disturbance. Faulty learning results in people making incorrect inferences on the basis of *inadequate or incorrect information* and failing to distinguish between imagination and reality. Beck does agree with Ellis that thinking may be unrealistic because it is based on unreasonable attitudes. The differences in the two therapies are mainly manifested in their goals and strategies. Rational emotive behavior therapy emphasizes a *basic philosophic change* in a person's belief system through disputation, while cognitive therapy focuses on the person's *perceptions of reality* and testing these perceptions empirically.

Rational Behavior Therapy

Rational behavior therapy (RBT), developed by psychiatrist Maxie Maultsby (1975), is philosophically very similar to rational emotive behavior therapy. The purpose of discussing RBT here is that it places considerable focus on self-instructional techniques which are referred to as rational self-analysis or rational self-counseling. Maultsby emphasizes the point that no method of counseling will work unless the client decides to *use* it. He further notes that we counsel ourselves daily, but unfortunately our self-counseling is often based on irrational thinking, and therefore works against us rather than for us. Finally he concludes "...the *only* effective counseling is self-counseling." What people therefore need is a good set of rules for deciding if their behavior is rational; and this is what rational self-counseling provides.

Rational self-counseling is a comprehensive self-help method that enables people to solve their personal problems with the rational use of their brain. As Maultsby states, "It deals directly with three main groups of habitual human behavior: habits of perceiving and thinking, or Cognitive behavior; habits of emotional feelings, or Emotive behaviors; and habits of voluntary action, or Physical behaviors."

Cognitive Behavior Modification

Cognitive behavior modification (Meichenbaum, 1977) emphasizes self-instructional training in much the same way as Maultsby. However, its focus is on changing an individual's self-talk rather than on teaching clients to question or challenge their thoughts *philosophically*.

Cognitive behavior modification teaches people new rational self-statements to replace their current dysfunctional statements. It does not, however, focus on the belief *system* nor does it attempt to bring about a basic philosophic change in one's belief system. Rather, it is based on the assumption that "inner talk" or "self-talk" in themselves have a powerful influence on behavior.

Cognitive behavior modification is a three-phase process. Phase one is self-observation. Before coming to therapy, the client's self-talk consists mainly of negative self-statements and images. At the beginning of therapy, clients' awareness is heightened by teaching them to focus on thoughts, feelings, physiological reactions, and interpersonal behaviors. Clients are taught to view their problems differently and to produce thoughts and behaviors that are incompatible with the maladaptive ones. In phase two, the clients' self-observations bring them to an inner dialogue which leads to a new conceptualization and ultimately to new methods of coping. In the third phase, clients are encouraged to engage in their new coping behaviors and focus on the self-talk they are experiencing when engaging in their new behaviors.

Interpersonal Cognitive Problem-Solving

Interpersonal cognitive problem-solving (Spivak, Platt & Schure, 1976) is another therapeutic approach which emphasizes cognitions as a major determinant of human behavior. Spivak and his colleagues posit that although people may learn to become less upset over the events of their life by changing their beliefs and attitudes, they often lack the *problem-solving skills* to significantly deal with these events. There seems to be no correlation between the ability to solve interpersonal problems and the ability to solve problems of a practical nature. However, there *is* a high correlation between a person's ability to handle everyday problems and his/her emotional well-being. It is *how* a person thinks rather than *what* he or she thinks that becomes the major determinant in a person's long range social success. According to Spivak, "In essence, a theory of cognitive problem-solving is being proposed that suggests that there is a grouping of interpersonal cognitive problem-solving (ICPS) skills that mediate the quality of our social adjustment." These skills are not significantly related to general intellectual ability, but are learned from experience in our culture.

Multi-Modal Behavior Therapy

In this final section on cognitive behavioral approaches, we shall discuss multi-modal behavior therapy, an approach developed by Arnold Lazarus after years of research and study of a wide range of therapeutic approaches. It logically belongs here because it represents what Lazarus (1976) calls a "creative synthesis." Multi-modal therapists view themselves as "...pragmatists who endorse scientific empiricism and logical positivism...". While Lazarus claims that "as multi-modal therapists we do not subscribe to any particular theory," he goes on to say that "our findings and observations do have a plan in a broad theoretical framework. This lies within the province of learning principles and, more especially, social learning, cognitive processes, and behavioral principles for which there is experimental evidence. We assume that a major portion of therapy is educational, and that the questions of how and why people learn and unlearn adaptive and maladaptive responses are crucial for effective therapeutic intervention."

Multi-modal behavior therapy describes humans as moving, feeling, sensing, imagining, thinking and relating. Each of these functions interacts with the others to create a total psychological profile; changing any one function will affect every other dimension. When a psychological disturbance is present, each area is affected and therefore complete therapy involves treating all modalities. Lazarus refers to behavior, affect, sensation, imagery, cognition and interpersonal processes as the six modalities that constitute human "personality," and he considers them the mainstay of psychology. However, he points out that the non-psychological modalities of neurological and biochemical factors should not be ignored since they obviously influence behavior, affective responses, sensations, images, cognitions, and interpersonal responses. He therefore added D (for drugs) to create his "BASIC-ID" acronym.

Multi-modal behavior therapy provides a comprehensive, systematic assessment and treatment model. Its emphasis on a thorough diagnostic survey using BASIC ID provides therapists with a complete profile of the client's functioning and avoids the common pitfall of focusing only on the favored approach of the particular therapist.

The Synergy of the Theories Combined

Rational effectiveness training (RET) incorporates aspects of the theories we have discussed in its model for workplace implementation. RET's emphasis on recognizing underlying beliefs means that its main focus is on assisting employees to develop productive attitudes through changing *demands* to *preferences,* resulting in fewer negative emotions when unpleasant events occur.

Drawing from cognitive theory, RET teaches individuals to change their inaccurate perceptions and interpretations of situations by focusing on facts rather than distortions. Rational behavior therapy adds the technique of rational emotive imagery and the "camera check" to assist participants in achieving a calmer and more logical approach to unpleasant experiences. Cognitive behavior modification's use of coping self-statements is incorporated to assist people in reducing their emotional disturbance so they can focus and complete tasks more effectively. By understanding the contributions of these various theories, the rational effectiveness trainer is better equipped to develop flexible approaches for helping participants achieve their goals.

CHAPTER 5

Toward an Integrated Training Approach

Social Skills Programs

Wendy, a telephone installation and repair specialist, has been suffering from stomach upsets and ulcers. When her doctor questioned her about possible sources of stress, she admitted that she was afraid to speak up to her co-workers and, as a result, she felt she was being "pushed around." She confided that she sometimes chewed the skin off her lip while she worked, so angry did she become at herself for letting others dump unfavorable assignments on her.

Her company offered an assertiveness training program and, following her physician's advice, she signed up for it. It was a classic assertiveness training program where, through role-plays and skills practice, Wendy learned a new repertoire of assertive behavioral stances.

Feeling stronger, she went back to the job and, sure enough, stood up to her co-workers when they attempted to give her drudge work. She applied everything she learned, and her amazed co-workers backed off.

But Wendy's stomach upset didn't go away. In fact, her distress became more acute.

Traditional assertiveness training often fails because it does not deal with the underlying emotions, especially anger and anxiety. A good assertiveness training program incorporating RET first asks the participant, "How do you *feel* about this?" These feelings are functions of certain thoughts. When the irrational thinking is replaced with positive self-talk, the emotions will no longer sabotage the learning of new assertive behavior.

In Wendy's case, she had been brought up to believe that others wouldn't like her unless she went along with them. After her assertiveness course, she applied the correct behavior but still felt anxious because her belief system—that it would be awful if others dislike her if she rocks the boat—had remained unchanged. This irrational belief blocked her from feeling non-anxious when behaving in an assertive manner.

Cognitive Training and Technical Skills Programs

Lowell, a speechwriter and public relations advisor to the president of a large paper company, has kept an old Underwood typewriter at his side for as long as anyone can remember. All of the secretaries have been using word processing for ten years, and recently the president said to Lowell, "Get with the program. That old antique is slowing us all down. I've signed you up for a one-week training course in word processing skills. Be there Monday morning."

A high strung but creative type, Lowell ran right down to the EAP office with a stress attack. He confided that he didn't think he could learn word processing. "I'm old enough to be the grandfather of everyone else in the class, and they'll all laugh at me. I'll never be able to face them if I fail the course."

For Lowell, learning new skills was blocked by his ideas

about failing and the accompanying anxiety. This kind of fear almost always hinders the learning process.

As organizations change, people frequently move into new positions which require new skills. Learning these skills means making mistakes and failing. Resistance to change and fear of failure go together. New learning experiences are hindered and blocked by fear and anxiety. Cognitive training teaches employees to deal with their inhibiting ideas and emotions so they can learn the new skills and organizational change can proceed smoothly.

Cognitive Training and Stress Management

High levels of stress over a long period of time are unhealthy and unproductive, and one of the main reasons for absenteeism and loss of productivity.

Stress is a popular but loosely-used concept. Most stress consists of a collection of strong emotions such as anger, fear, and depression. Early detection of these feelings, and learning how to identify their source and reduce their intensity and duration, are one way of managing the problem. But what is *causing* the strong emotions? And why do different people react differently to the same stressors? An impatient and aggressive boss, for example, makes some people nervous; yet others stay calm and relatively relaxed.

According to stress researcher Richard Lazarus, the difference between individuals' reactions is mainly caused by differences in their *appraisal and coping strategies*. Only extremely strong stressors like war, serious illness, and the death of a loved one cause stress phenomena in large groups of people.

The milder stressors—those found in most organizations—include unclear tasks, not being rewarded for results, interpersonal conflicts, and an unclear picture of the company's goals and objectives. These can lead to very different reactions, depending on the individual's belief systems and coping skills.

Dr. Browning, an internist, is well known for her unclear orders and aggressive outbursts at the nurses in her ward. One of the head nurses, Debbie, feels angry and frustrated by these incidents. When she goes home she feels depressed and exhausted. Rose, the head nurse of the neighboring ward, is also confronted with Dr. Browning's ambiguous behavior. While Rose sometimes gets irritated, in general she is able to manage the situation by asking specific questions and largely ignoring Dr. Browning's rude behavior. She keeps calm and makes the best of it. She is calm enough to go on and ask for more information, whereas Debbie is too upset to get the details and spends a lot of energy upsetting herself.

Debbie tells herself, "This doctor *shouldn't* treat me this way," and "Female doctors especially should be courteous to nurses." These irrational beliefs cause feelings of anger. She is also telling herself that "I am a weakling by accepting this behavior." This negative evaluation of herself then causes her to feel demeaned and depressed.

Rose, on the other hand, tells herself, "I definitely don't like this rude behavior, but I know I can't change it. So I'm just going to make the best of it." By accepting reality she is able to stay calm and to cope with the same stressor in a more adequate way than Debbie.

Demanding that people behave differently and condemning oneself for one's shortcomings are some of the major causes of stress. In teaching people to manage their stress, the trainer first needs to deal with the irrational beliefs causing the emotional disturbance.

To be effective, a stress management program has to deal in a multi-leveled way with cognitive, feeling, and behavioral components. Other important coping skills for stress management include relaxation skills, assertiveness training, and time management.

Training in Leadership Skills

Training programs in leadership skills deal with topics like planning and controlling production, motivating people, and learning how to delegate. The management culture of the last decade has been preoccupied with managers feeling respected and subordinates feeling warmly toward them. Modern management philosophies stress the emotional components of the relationship between the manager and his co-workers. This "love philosophy" can create uncertainty with managers and impede the decision–making process, because the manager is stymied by such thoughts as "How will my people react? Will all of them still like and respect me?"

Indecision can also result from a belief in The Perfect Decision—that among all the alternatives, there is one right and perfect solution. Meeting after meeting is held, decisions are postponed, while waiting and working for the perfect solution.

The underlying irrational beliefs are, "If I make the wrong decision, it will show I'm a rotten manager" and "Life, and business, should be predictable; I cannot tolerate the unknown."

But of course a manager must execute many unpopular activities, such as discipline, correcting mistakes, writing job evaluations, and giving orders. *To be effective, it is crucial that a leadership training program deal with the belief system of the participants.*

Organizational Change

When organizations change, people are required to take on new responsibilities and learn new skills. When a company is taken over by another, new bosses and new policies have to be adjusted to, as happens when an employee is transferred to a new department or a new part of the country. New technical skills are required on an ongoing basis.

Emotions such as anxiety and anger cause resistance to change. Rigid irrational beliefs such as "It would be terrible if I fail in this new position," accompanied by disaster fantasies and thoughts such as "It is unfair; my position in this company should be guaranteed for life," cause these strong emotions. It is this emotional resistance that gets the organization stuck in a quagmire.

If a company's human resources are taught to cope in a realistic way with the new requirements, and they are not afraid of making mistakes when confronted with new tasks, they can actually feel challenged and energized by change.

Only companies with a flexible and adaptive culture can survive the continuing demands of the marketplace. Teaching rational thinking skills is therefore an excellent long-term investment in the survival of the company.

CHAPTER 6

The Format of the Training Program

In the pre-training phase, steps have to be taken to translate the needs of the company into a workable and effective program. Usually, this process involves representatives from the company such as the Human Resources or Personnel Department, the Training/Education Department and/or the Health/Wellness Department and potential participants, trainers and consultants. Participation from these major players helps facilitate the process of agreeing on and reaching goals.

Before designing a Rational Effectiveness Training program, it is advisable to go through the following steps:

1. *Identify the issues* that face the participants: e.g., stress-related complaints; absenteeism; unsatisfactory interpersonal relations in the department.

2. *Determine the goals* of the participants and their employers, such as "increasing stress management capabilities" and "developing more effective communication."

3. Consider the *behavioral, emotional* and *cognitive components* which interfere with their attaining their goals. For example:

   Behavioral goals: Reducing avoidance of conflicts

and increasing assertiveness.

Emotional goals: Reducing employee frustration, anger and anxiety

Cognitive goals:

- Reducing demandingness about the "perfect organization" and the "perfect boss;"
- Reducing managers' intolerance of mistakes;
- Dispelling exaggerated fantasies about the consequences of speaking up to colleagues and superiors.

4. *Analyze the interrelationships between these three components,* starting with the behavioral component.

- Are the emotions responsible for the ineffective behavior?
- If so, hypothesize the irrational beliefs that could play an important role in causing the emotions.

  Example: *Avoidance of conflicts* and *lack of assertiveness* are caused by *anxiety* and suppressed *anger.*

  Anxiety may be caused by irrational ideas about the consequences of expressing one's desires or showing imperfection. There may also be a *secondary* problem, such as fearful fantasies of what is going to happen if angry feelings are expressed. Angry feelings may be associated with perfectionistic demands about the organization and the boss.

The resulting training proposal may include behavioral, cognitive, and emotive elements such as:

- RET sessions on reducing anger and anxiety
- Behavioral exercises in communication and assertiveness

• Relaxation training.

The RET Influence

In the remainder of this chapter we will focus on developing the RET component of the program. An RET workshop typically has the following outline:

1. Introductory exercises
2. Mini-lecture on the "ABC's"
3. Differentiating rational from irrational beliefs
4. Demonstration of disputing techniques
5. Disputation in small groups
6. Homework assignments

1. Introductory Exercises

Example: Fear of criticism

Begin the training by eliciting some common experience which generates thoughts and feelings on the subject of criticism in the workplace. You may want to suggest an issue. For example, "You are on your way to see your supervisor. Serious mistakes were made in your department, and you will be blamed for the errors."

The trainer processes the experiences of the participants by explaining the similarities and differences of the feelings as a result of the issue. The trainer interviews different members to show the beliefs and thoughts connected with individual feelings, posing such questions as "What were you thinking as you imagined yourself walking to the supervisor's office?"

In the first part of the group session, the trainer's aim is to demonstrate the following points:

1. When confronted with the same situation, different people can experience different emotions.

2. Different *emotions* are linked to different *thoughts*.

2. Introducing the RET Model

The trainer explains the RET model and illustrates it with several examples from the first exercise, the trainer's own experience, and from the information collected in the pre-training phase.

Teaching people to discriminate between actual events (A), thoughts (B), feelings and behaviors (C) is an important goal of this part of the session. For most people the selection of events is very difficult because of their inability to clearly distinguish between *feelings* and *thoughts*. They may, for example, say "I *feel* I'm being misused" instead of "I *think* I'm being misused and therefore I *feel* angry."

This lecture and group discussion has several goals:

• To teach participants to discriminate between facts (A), thoughts (B), and feelings and resulting behaviors (C).

• To demonstrate to group members the "B→C connection" (the connection between beliefs and feeling) as opposed to their accustomed "A-C" (event→ feeling). "Emotions are not caused be events that occur but rather by your thoughts about these events."

3. Rational and Irrational Beliefs

The trainer gives an overview of the main irrational beliefs that can cause various self-defeating emotional reactions and poor performance, such as perfectionism, low frustration tolerance and demandingness. The irrational beliefs that are directly related to the workshop goals are to be emphasized for the participants.

A clear and ongoing demonstration of the difference between irrational and rational beliefs remains a common theme throughout the training.

For example, "My colleague behaves badly" is a rational belief only if the next part of the sentence, "he shouldn't do it," is an irrational idea. Most of the time the second or irrational part is implicit. The trainer's role is to help the client to speak the implicit part of the message by questioning the rational versus irrational thoughts followed by teaching the difference in the emotional and behavioral consequences.The main goal of this part of the session is to teach participants how *irrational* thoughts lead to self-defeating feelings and behavior, and *rational* thoughts lead to non-self-defeating feelings and behavior

4. Demonstration of Disputation Techniques

In the next phase of the workshop the trainer demonstrates how people can change their unproductive irrational ideas by the *disputing* process. The main question to ask when disputing irrational beliefs is: *"What is the empirical evidence that supports this belief?"*

Sample Irrational Belief (IB): "If I give a poor presentation, it will ruin my career and my life will be useless."

Question by trainer: "Even if you are right that it's the end of your career (which is improbable but possible), where is the evidence that your life has no use anymore? Let's look at the possibility of living a meaningful life without this specific career."

A second important question to ask is: "Does this belief *help* you in achieving your goals of delivering a good presentation and pursuing a successful career?"

If the participant sees the irrationality and the destructiveness of her thinking and is able to formulate a rational version of the belief, it's time for the next question: "How would you feel if you could tell yourself 'Even if I fail with this presentation, and even if it leads to the end of my career, I can lead a meaningful life'?"

If the client can accept this belief and sees the advantages of this way of thinking, move to another example.

It is important to spend adequate time demonstrating disputing techniques in the group, because they are an essential part of convincing the participants of the usefulness of the RET cognitive change techniques.

5. Disputation in Small Groups

After participating in large group exercises, it is important for the group members to work individually on practicing self-observation and disputation techniques. An RET self-help form can be a very useful device in that it enables participants to more clearly identify their own specific irrational beliefs.

Begin by instructing trainees to work individually for 10–15 minutes on completing their form. Next, divide the group into triads and instruct them how to help each other in making their irrational beliefs more explicit and then disputing them. The subgroup exercise takes 45 minutes, with the trainer moving between subgroups to give assistance where needed.

After the triads have finished, process the exercise in the

large group and encourage questions about anything that may not be clear.

6. Homework Assignments

Regular practice is a crucial element in RET because beliefs and ways of thinking are products of long-term learning. Newer, more rational ways of thinking are best achieved when there is intensive practice outside the group both between sessions and after the workshop ends. Homework assignments are an indispensible part of the program. Typical RET homework assignments are:

- monitoring
- disputing exercises
- shame-attacking exercises
- practicing rational coping statements
- rational emotive imagery

Monitoring

It is important that self observation precede cognitive change. Monitoring thoughts during typical incidents in real life is a first step in discovering the irrational thoughts and beliefs causing the disturbing emotions. A between-session homework assignment can be "write down as specifically as possible the events preceding the disturbing emotion and ineffective behavior along with your thoughts"— in other words, have them put their problems into the "ABC" framework.

Disputing Exercises

Once participants are able to recognize the thoughts and

beliefs causing their self-defeating feelings and behavior, and have practiced disputing them in the group, the next step is to train them to dispute their irrational beliefs outside the group. They are given a series of questions to help them in the disputing process: 1) How is this belief helping me? Hurting me? 2) Where is the evidence for the truth of this belief? 3) Is it logical?

"Shame-Attacking" Exercises

Participants are instructed to do something in real life they consider extremely shameful or embarrassing. The goal is to test the reality of their fantasies about behaving foolishly and being ridiculed. At the same time it gives them the opportunity to practice disputing the catastrophizing beliefs about potentially negative events.

Examples:

- A woman who is very preoccupied with her looks is instructed to wear hair curlers in the train on her way to the training program.

- A perfectionistic group member is instructed to do something stupid in public such as asking foolish or incomprehensible questions.

Practicing Rational Coping Statements

A major goal of rational effectiveness training is for trainees to develop rational thoughts which enable them to cope in more effective ways with daily situations. Once insight and self-knowledge have occurred, the next step is to practice the new ways of thinking in daily life. Homework assignments aimed at practicing the new thinking habits are an essential part of the training program.

A common homework assignment is to visualize a difficult situation three times a day while practicing rational coping statements to help reduce any potential anger, anxiety, or self-downing.

Rational Emotive Imagery

Rational Emotive Imagery (REI) is a procedure used to elucidate and practice rational thinking. The participant is asked to imagine the problematic situation and to make himself as disturbed as possible about it. If the person succeeds, the next instruction is to "lower the intensity of the feeling without changing the situation." In the process of doing this, many participants discover helpful rational coping thoughts. After REI has been demonstrated in the group, it can be practiced daily to strengthen rational thinking and lower the intensity of the disturbed feelings while imagining the difficult event. This exercise can be very convincing for many participants as it provides a direct experience of how emotional control can be achieved by changing thoughts.

7. Disputing strategies

As we have seen, the trainer's role is to help trainees to recognize their irrational ways of thinking and to show them ways to change them. The most frequently used strategy for changing irrational beliefs is called *disputing*. Ellis introduced this method, also known as "the Socratic dialogue," in the 1950's. The Greek philosopher Socrates used to teach by asking his pupils questions in such a way as to encourage them to think more logically and philosophically. In RET this questioning method is used as a strategy to help people examine their views of the world and themselves and to correct faulty and disturbed ways of thinking.

Several different disputational techniques can be employed. In *philosophical disputation,* the goal is to question the beliefs one has about one's life and the world: "If you do something stupid, how does it make you a totally worthless person?" In *empirical disputation* you examine the correctness of your interpretations of events by collecting data: "Is it really true that everybody hates you for what you did? Let us look at the evidence." In *functional disputation* you are questioning the utility of certain beliefs in helping reach your goals: "If you think your speech will be a disaster, how does that help you to improve your speech?"

In the following dialogues between trainer and trainee, the application of these different disputation strategies are demonstrated.

Fred is the head of a department who has problems in getting along with co-workers. In his yearly performance appraisal, Fred was told of numerous complaints from his co-workers about his aggressive outbursts at them. It was recommended that he sign up for a course in Communication Skills for Managers.

During the training program, the trainer and Fred develop the following ABC analysis of a typical incident:

A (Activating event): Fred's secretary, Rita, promised to type an important 10-page productivity report by Thursday afternoon so he could have it in time for a Friday 8:30 a.m. management meeting. At 5:00 on Thursday afternoon, he discovers that the report is not ready, and sees that Rita is about to leave. When he asks about the report, she says: "I'm sorry but there were so many other important things I had to do, I couldn't finish it. And I absolutely have to leave now."

B (Irrational beliefs): Who does she think she is? A secretary *should* follow my instructions. We agreed upon this; there is no reason why she shouldn't have finished it.

C (Emotional and behavioral Consequences): Anger; shouting at Rita and threatening her with dismissal.

A. Philosophical Disputation

Trainer: I agree this behavior of Rita's is very irritating. But why *must* she keep her promises at all times? People sometimes don't, unfortunately.

Fred: But she *never* keeps her promises. She makes her own schedule as it suits her, and that's that.

Trainer: Let's suppose you are right. Most of the time she doesn't keep her promises. Explain to me what law of the universe says she *must* not act this way? Especially now that you know it's one of her typical characteristics!

Fred: Because I want her to do this and I'm her boss.

Trainer: You are saying that just because you *want* it, she *must* do it even though you know that many times she in fact does not. Where is it written that other people *should* behave according to your rules and demands—even when you *are* the boss? You may be the boss; but can you rule the universe and the behavior of its inhabitants?

Fred: I agree, of course, that Rita can do what she wants. But it's extremely annoying to me when she leaves me in the lurch.

Trainer: Of course it's annoying when Rita doesn't keep her promises. But people have flaws, and this seems to be pretty clearly one of hers. It's rational to *prefer* employees meet deadlines. But do you see that it is irrational to expect that other people *always* do what you want, merely because you want it?

Fred: You're right—it is a bit irrational to expect this.

Trainer: What could you tell yourself next time someone doesn't do what you want—something that would make you feel irritated and annoyed instead of angry?

B. Empirical Disputation

Trainer: Why does Rita fail to meet deadlines?

Fred: I think she is just lazy and doesn't bother.

Trainer: Let's talk about her laziness and her indifferent attitude. Is she *always* like this?

Fred: No, not always; but she is very strict about going home at 5:30—even when there is still important work to be completed.

Trainer: Do you have any idea what her reason is for leaving at 5:30?

Fred: Maybe she wants to be at home in time for her children.

Trainer: You could say she's very responsible for the children at these moments. She obviously gives high priority to her family. Isn't it therefore a bit of an over generalization to say she is lazy and indifferent? It might be more accurate to say she may not plan very well and that she sometimes gives too much priority to her private life.

Fred: Maybe you're right. But still, when she doesn't keep her promises about such a crucial project, it is extremely annoying.

Trainer: Of course, the annoying facts still exist. But how would you feel if you could tell yourself, "This is annoying; at this moment her priorities are incorrect and she didn't plan very well. But it's not because she is lazy or indifferent—just a fallible human being"?

Fred: I guess I'd feel less angry and have an easier time talking to her without shouting.

C. Functional Disputation

Trainer: Has it worked for you, when you think "She *should* always keep her appointments"? Has it helped you reach your goal?

Fred: No, the relationship in fact has been getting worse and worse. Sometimes she doesn't even listen to me anymore because she's so angry at me.

Trainer: And does it help *you* when you make yourself so angry?

Fred: I don't like it. When I come home afterwards I'm still feeling tense and maybe even guilty.

Trainer: So this way of thinking not only doesn't work for you; to the contrary—it actually has *negative* effects. Let's talk about some strategies that might work better for you in accomplishing your goals.

CHAPTER 7

Coping with Resistance During Training

Resistant behavior is very common in all kinds of training programs. Participants are sometimes not very responsive: they don't follow instructions, they're late to the sessions, they keep arguing in unproductive ways, they forget their homework assignments, and find all kinds of pretexts to derail the training experience.

Trainers tend to consider behaviors which are non-productive according to the training goals as *resistance*. Some blame the resistant participant rather than analyzing the problem and working out strategies to overcome the resistance. Because coping with resistance is a very important part of the professional trainer's job, we choose to stress an interactional viewpoint that recognizes resistant behavior as a normal part of the relationship between trainer and trainee.

The Working Contract

The most common cause of resistance is a lack of agreement between trainer and participants on why a difficult task, such as changing one's ideas, can serve the participant's goals.

The first task of the trainer is to convince the trainee of the positive relationship between changing ideas and more productive emotions and behavior. People are likely to start working on change only if they can see how it can benefit them in reaching their own goals.

Edward Bordin and Windy Dryden put forward the concept of the *working alliance,* a classic psychoanalytical concept that can be very useful in analyzing the relationship between trainer and trainee. According to Bordin, the strength of the working alliance is the key factor in the change process. An effective working alliance is determined by three main factors: agreement on *goals,* agreement on *tasks,* and agreement on *bonds.*

Agreement on Goals

People take part in training programs for a number of reasons. They want to lessen their wretched feelings of stress, they want to be more successful in handling their employees, or they want to be winning negotiators. The RET trainer's task is to teach the trainees how to think in more rational, productive and less disturbing ways. Trainees will be motivated to change their way of thinking only if they can see its relevance in reaching their own goals. Thinking rationally is, in fact, only a *sub-goal* on the road to the main goal of the participant. Only if there is an implicit or explicit agreement on working on this sub-goal, and an understanding of its relevance to the participant's major goals, will the trainee be motivated. The perfectionist will likely work on unrealistic demands only if she can see that her performance will be the same or better with less energy if the demands are given up. The angry negotiator wants to work on his demanding beliefs only if he sees that by giving up these beliefs the chances of winning through negotiation can be accomplished.

Agreement on Tasks

Trainees are expected to do all kinds of things in training: reading, role-playing, explaining details about their jobs, describing their feelings and thoughts, and disputing their irrational ideas. To the trainer, these tasks are very familiar and he clearly understands the relevance to the trainees' stated goals. But what about the trainees? Is it really surprising when they object to role-playing, when they don't see how a simulated office dialogue connects to their real-life emotions in the workplace?

Only when people can understand how performing these difficult and uncomfortable tasks can help them reach their goals will they be motivated to do them. Another question the trainer would better ask herself is, "Is this task too difficult?" For many people, giving specific descriptions of thoughts and feelings is something very new. They are not used to introspection, they may not have the verbal skills, and they may be painfully uncomfortable. In other words, the trainer is expecting the trainee to do something he never learned. In this case, learning self-observation skills would better be the first sub-goal to be worked on.

Only if trainees clearly understand the relevance of these tasks to their longer-range goals can they be reasonably expected to put energy into them. And, of course, the level of difficulty has to be within the range of the trainee's ability.

Agreement on Bonds

People differ in their preferred learning approaches. Some people learn better when they discover for themselves what their irrational ideas are. Others learn better when they're told directly what's wrong with their ideas. Preferred learning styles can come from the individual's idiosyncrasies; often, the preference is influenced by the cultural background of the participants. People from Turkey, for example, are much more used to experts like doctors and teachers who tell them right away what to do instead of inviting them to join in examining the causes of the unproductive behavior. Adjustment to the individual's learning style can greatly enhance the trainer-trainee relationship.

Who Is the Actual Contract Partner?

In training program, often the only agreement that exists is between the trainer or the consulting firm and the employer. Typically, the mandate is, "Teach the people in my department or my company how to improve their (selling skills) (negotiating skills) (management skills)." A clear agreement between trainer and participants on the above dimensions has to be reached in the training itself or in an orientation procedure before the training starts. Developing a helpful working contract between trainer and the participants is an ongoing process with several steps:

- Provide clear, *written information* for participants before the training starts. Explain the specific goals of the training and how it can benefit them in their own work. Give examples of the kinds of exercises they can expect and explain your role as a trainer.

- For longer programs, group or individual orientation or intake procedures are recommended to clarify what will be going on in the training and to assist the participants in formulating their individual learning goals.

- During your introduction, relate the goals and tasks in your program to the daily work of the participants so they can see how they will benefit from it.

- Be as clear as possible about your own role in the program; e.g., facilitator, teacher who provides information and models, socratic questioner, etc.

- Try to be sensitive to the different learning styles of individuals in the group. Some people expect straight answers to their questions, some prefer to be helped to discover their own answers, others prefer active exercises.

Intervention Power

Resistance and lack of motivation are also influenced by the trainer's performance, especially by the way he or she presents the material and gets and keeps the trainee's attention.

Interventions will be impactful and lead to learning only if there is sufficient attention paid by participants to the presented material. The psychological literature suggests that attention depends on two interdependent factors: the *strength of the stimulus* and the *level of arousal of the subjects*. In training programs, several strategies can be used to build up intervention power:

- Keep arousal at a high level by using drama in the presentation: e.g., accentuate the message by selective pauses, raising your voice, using gestures, etc. Or create high expectations of benefit: "In this exercise something *very* important will happen."

- The impact of the same types of interventions becomes weaker by repetition. You can work against this phenomenon, known as "habituation," by using a variety of techniques, such as verbal and nonverbal exercises or imagery techniques. You can also use highly evocative interventions: "If this (irrational idea) is true, then why not just expect to be miserable the rest of your life?" Or

"Why don't you buy a machine gun if your boss is such
a monster?"

• Most of the time, experiential exercises are more likely
to generate stronger experiences and higher levels of
arousal than exercises that simply deal with basic here-
and-now events.

• By giving interesting homework assignments between
sessions, when working with individuals or with groups,
you will be able to maintain participants' engagement
and interest in the training.

• From social psychology we are familiar with the
"Hawthorne effect." Presenting the training program as
something very special—"a new method" or "a program
the whole company is looking at"—often creates
expectancy of benefit and therefore improves the motivation of the trainees.

Indirect Strategies for Coping with Resistance.

Direct strategies for coping with resistance, such as
disputing irrational ideas causing resistance, explaining the
relevance of the program to the trainees' own goals, or using
more dramatic interventions, sometimes just don't seem to
work. Trying directly to convince participants often provokes
even *more* resistance, especially if there is a lot of ambivalence
towards the training program or towards certain exercises.
Listen to the following dialogue between a trainer and a
trainee who refuses to take part in a role playing exercise. His
arguments against role playing are that "It's not real;" but his
nonverbal signals show that underlying this protest is a lot
of fear.

Trainee: By doing this skit in the group, it just isn't

the same as the feelings I get when the situation actually happens in the office.

Trainer: I know from my experience that people can feel emotions very much like they do in reality when simulating situations.

Trainee: This colleague at my office is so weird, nobody could ever imitate him. (Etc.)

Direct trainer interventions could include: insisting on the working contract ("Role playing is part of the program, as we agreed upon") or providing more arguments supporting the usefulness of the role-playing method.

In the case above, an *indirect* strategy of coping with the resistance would probably work more effectively. You might, for example, fully agree with the resister and even exaggerate the problem. "I think you're right. Your problem with this colleague is so serious that absolutely nothing can be done about it, and maybe you're just going to have to accept this reality."

Another way to challenge the trainee is to question her abilities: "I think it's too early for you to do any role playing; today you'd better just observe others in the group."

Lange (1987) and Rabkin (1977) describe many examples of these "judo-like" strategies of dealing with resistant behavior in therapeutic relationships.

The following are some examples of "judo" strategies that can be used in training settings:

• In the pre-training interview, a trainee expresses his doubts about the usefulness of the training. The trainer gives as much information as possible and ends the interview with, "Don't make a decision now. It's very important for you to take your time and talk to colleagues and your supervisor before you make your mind up."

- During a session, the trainer is disputing somebody's perfectionistic demands. The trainee keeps defending her idea that "It's just not acceptable to me to make mistakes." The trainer finishes the dispute by telling her: "Maybe the best thing for you to do *is* to go on maintaining this demand on yourself the rest of your life, and just learn to accept the consequences—like your chronic anxiety about failing."

- In formulating homework assignments for a resistant client, the trainer can offer a choice between two alternatives: "I see two ways for you to work on this problem. Either you could do a shame-attacking exercise by asking foolish questions in your meetings, or you could do written disputes of your anxiety-producing beliefs in the meetings. Which do you prefer?" This strategy is based on Erickson's choice principle, whereby instead of offering the alternatives of "homework or no homework," the trainer offers a choice between two kinds of comparable homework assignments, thus making the third alternative (doing nothing) less probable!

- The trainer's intention is to introduce some imagery exercises, but she is dubious about the motivation of some of the trainees. Instead of introducing and convincing them, she thinks aloud: "I could do some special exercises now, but I think they won't suit you," implying that it's too difficult for this group. When the trainer changes the subject, some of the group members' interest may be piqued and they will ask the trainer, "Tell us more about this exercise." Only after they keep asking does the trainer (reluctantly) agree to do the exercise.

The core of these "judo" strategies is to acknowledge and "join the resistance," instead of fighting it. The resister is placed in a position in which he can resist by compliance.

Irrational Beliefs Causing Resistance

Resistance to change in training programs is, according to RET, caused by the same irrational beliefs that cause other kinds of unproductive emotions and behavior. Ideas connected with low frustration tolerance, such as "I can't *stand* performing these difficult tasks" or "life *should* be easy," lead to avoidance behavior and frustrated feelings. Most of the time, it is these ideas that are at the core of the resistance in groups. The symptoms include such statements as, "I tried but it didn't work. This is not the right method for me," "I understand it rationally but my feelings don't change," or insisting on easy solutions ("Just tell me what to do instead of this complicated disputing stuff"). This LFT philosophy—demanding easy changes and instant cures—is fueled by the hyped-up flyers selling one- or two-day workshops that purport to "change your life."

The trainer needs to keep emphasizing with the trainees how difficult (yet possible) it is to change ideas they have been reinforcing for decades and how unrealistic it is for them to expect major changes after only a few trials. An important direct way of coping with resistance is therefore to analyze the resistant behavior, translate it into ABC terms, and show participants how to vigorously and persistently dispute the irrationality of their underlying beliefs. Then, the other major RET strategies, such as coping statements like "No gain without pain" or "By trying, I have a better chance than by doing nothing," or doing repeated rational-emotive imagery to reduce dysfunctional emotions, can be used by participants to work on their low frustration tolerance.

CHAPTER 8

Self-Management for Trainers

Trainers' reactions can be as self-defeating and unproductive as many of the reactions of their participants. Feelings of anger, insecurity, disappointment, guilt, and over-confidence may be a few of the self-defeating and unproductive reactions experienced by the trainer during the introduction of a new program.

By using RET to manage their own emotions and inflexible or unproductive behavior, trainers become more effective role models for the group. Thus, personal mastery of RET skills and techniques becomes an integral part of trainers' expertise in helping *others* to correct their irrational ideas.

Like the swimming teacher who must be a good swimmer, RET trainers need to be able to successfully apply RET techniques to their own unproductive reactions in order to provide a solid educational and experiential program.

Let's consider some examples of common emotions and behaviors in the life of the average trainer.

The Angry Trainer

Example: One of the participants refuses to participate in role-playing exercises. He also tries to convince *others* in the group not to take part. "It's not the real thing," he complains. "In real life, everything is totally different." The trainer feels angry and starts lecturing the participant, whose resistance increases while his colleagues chime in and defend him.

The underlying *irrational belief* of the trainer is "People should behave the way I want them to behave and I can't stand it when they don't cooperate."

A more *rational belief,* such as "people have the right to view things differently—it's a pity, but that's reality," would result in less disturbing emotions for the trainer. It will also increase the likelihood that participants will at least experiment with role- playing.

The Insecure Trainer

Example: One of the participants in the management training program has a skeptical look on her face while listening to the lecture on quality improvement programs. She is a member of the committee that's going to make the decision regarding the program. The lecturer, who is one of the developers of the program, starts feeling very anxious. Instead of talking fluently to the group, he sticks rigidly to his written text.

His *underlying irrational beliefs (IB's)*: "Everybody must like my proposals. If not, I've failed and something terrible is going to happen."

A more *rational belief* would be: "I can accept the possibility that this important person doesn't agree with me and doesn't like my ideas. If this is true and my proposals are not accepted, then it's too bad, but not awful. I'll survive the critics and the refusal. I'd better think of another way to reach my goals." The effect of this more rational attitude would be less anxiety, a more flexible and relaxed performance, and a higher probability of acceptance by the critics.

The Training Failure

Example: Most of the group members rate the 2-day Social Skills Training rather negatively. There is a high probability there will not be follow-up programs because of the low ratings. The trainer loses self-confidence and enthusiasm.

Her *underlying irrational beliefs (IB's):* "I'm no good as a trainer. I'll always fail. I am a failure and worthless."

A more *rational belief* would be: "I failed to do a good job in this particular training. It shows I am fallible—as *all* humans are. And I very much regret there will not be a follow-up program. Now how can I learn from the mistakes I made so that next time I can prevent them from happening again?" This kind of rational attitude would not only lead to a less disturbing emotion, but also to a more constructive *problem-solving* approach for improving one's presentation skills.

The Guilty Trainer

Example: One group member seems to have lots of personal problems. She keeps trying to bring them up in the group, but the trainer stops her because they are off the track of the training. The group member leaves right after the session. One of the other participants tells the trainer that this group member feels very disappointed because she expected more attention and solutions for her personal problems. The trainer feels very guilty and gives ample opportunity in the next session to bring up personal problems.

Irrational beliefs (IB): "I should have treated this individual in a better way. I'm a bad leader."

A more *rational belief* in this situation would be: "Maybe it would have been better if I had given this person more time to talk about her personal problems. Maybe I was too fast in cutting her off. If I had given more attention to her problem, I could have explained to her that it was beyond the scope of the training session without hurting her feelings. Next time I think I'll try that. For now, however, I can accept myself with my mistakes, without condemning myself as a person."

The Manic Trainer

Example: The evaluation ratings of the training program are excellent. The participants learned a lot of relevant skills, plus they were very satisfied with the way the training was presented. The trainer feel great. She is very self-confident, and nothing on earth can destroy this successful feeling. She considers herself a *great trainer.*

Irrational beliefs (IB): "Now I know I can do anything. I am a total success as a trainer and as a person."

A more *rational belief* would be: "I really enjoyed how great I did in this training. There is a good chance I'll be successful with training programs. But I can also accept myself even when I get *negative* evaluations, which is always possible. Being successful at a certain *task* does not change my worth as an individual." This more realistic and less grandiose belief better prepares the trainer for inevitable failures in the future. Rating their *self-worth* by their successful *performances* makes people much more vulnerable to mistakes and failures.

Managing Your Own Emotions and Unproductive Behavior

Our advice to the professional trainer who is considering RET strategies is to work regularly on your own unproductive reactions by following this "Seven-Step Procedure for Self-management."

Step 1. Describe your problem situation *(A)*.

Example: Participants in my 2-day workshop give me bad ratings on my training. They consider it irrelevant and are very critical of my interventions as a trainer.

Step 2. List your self-defeating emotions and ineffective behaviors *(C)*.

I feel very *unmotivated* and *depressed*. I don't discuss the problem with my partner; I *isolate* myself.

Step 3. Formulate your main self-defeating thoughts and irrational beliefs *(IB's)*.

My underlying IB's are: "I'm no good as a trainer. I'll always fail. I am a failure and a worthless individual."

Step 4. Dispute your irrational beliefs (IB's).

"Where is the evidence?"

"Can I really not stand it?"

"How does doing a bad job this time make me a failure as a trainer and a worthless individual?"

"When I look at the facts I can accurately say only that I did poorly with this particular training, which is too bad. But it's an exaggeration to say that I *always* fail when in fact several of my past evaluations were positive. It is also very irrational to rate myself as a poor trainer because of one or two low-rated workshops. I'd better look at my performance on several occasions to get a measure of my performance as a *professional.* Then I can work out some ways to improve my skills. To rate myself as a worthless *individual* is even more nonsensical. As an individual, I have thousands of characteristics which I could measure and rate. I'd better accept myself as an ordinary fallible human being."

Step 5. Formulate more effective rational beliefs *(E)*.

"If I fail in doing my job, I don't like it. But I can use this experience to improve my skills and learn from my mistakes. If I tell this to myself I'll still feel *disappointed,* but it won't rob me of my energy to work on improving my professional skills."

Step 6. Test run! Go back to the problem situation *(A)* and do a rational emotive imagery exercise on it.

Imagine, for example, receiving a bad evaluation and being criticized, and keep repeating to yourself your new rational beliefs (Step 5). If you are feeling *disappointment* rather than *self-downing* or *depression,* you have probably replaced your *irrational* beliefs with an appropriate *rational* beliefs. If not, go back to steps (3) and (4) and start looking for other *IB's* that are at work and start disputing again.

Step 7. Formulate a plan of action for training yourself to change your ineffective and self-defeating beliefs. Be as specific as possible.

Example: "I'll do the imagery exercise twice a day for the next three weeks." Or "Every time I feel depressed I'll identify my IB's and dispute them." Or "Every workday this month, I'll rate the various aspects of my job performance to get a realistic image of my weaknesses and strengths." Or "I'll ask a colleague for feedback on my functioning as a trainer and suggestions on how to improve some of my deficient skills."

CHAPTER 9

How to "Sell" Your RET Program: Straight Talk from RET Professionals to Training Innovators

How can RET be effectively introduced to companies when there is so much competition around? Before you can effectively convince others that your program is worth contracting for, you have to be quite convinced yourself that this is a useful program and will definitely benefit the company. Before attempting to sell the program to others, sit down and list all the objections you think might be raised to the program. Are these aspects of the program that you are uncomfortable with? Why? Dispute any irrational beliefs you have that might interfere with your presentation. Be sure you do not have any internal resistance to the approach.

Also dispute your own belief that others *must* accept this program simply because *you* think it is useful. Resistance is part of the process. Listen to the criticisms and don't argue with the prospective buyer. Explain to them all the ways the training can benefit them. Ask them what their goals are in training and what are their frustrations. Then design a presentation that will show them how the RET program can help them achieve their goals and relieve their and their employees' frustrations. Introducing RET to others can be seen as a three-step process:

Step 1: Self-analysis. Explore your feelings and thoughts that interfere with your total acceptance of the approach. Dispute any old and rigid ideas you might have that keep you from accepting RET. Dispute your low frustration tolerance (LFT) and discomfort anxiety.

Step 2: Listen carefully to your buyer (your boss or a customer). Allow them time to express their frustrations and clarify their goals. Become as familiar as you can with the "company culture." Know the product line. Find out about the company's strategic plans. What are their fears?

Step 3: Develop an RET training program which will help your client achieve their goals and relieve their frustrations. In presenting the program, apply your RET skills to the buyers so that they can have a personal experience with how it works. Do not argue with them, but simply reinforce the importance of changing employees' self-defeating beliefs in order for the company to accomplish its goals.

Beware of Presenting Productivity Motivation as Therapy

What are some of the common issues you will be confronted with when trying to introduce Rational Effectiveness Training to potential clients? First, it is important to avoid any mention of "therapy." Although RET principles were originated for use in therapy, they are *principles of behavior change which can be used in a wide variety of settings*. Trainers are expected to produce programs which will increase productivity and motivation among employees. Rather than talking about "emotions" and "feelings," you would do better to use words and phrases such as "wasteful reactions" or "impulsive behavior." Clearly show the relationship between "wasteful reactions" and productivity. Every minute employees spend complaining about their job costs money. Show your prospective client how RET training provides employees with a method for changing wasteful reactions into productive responses.

The Competition

Often you will come across people in decision-making positions who are rigidly committed to another approach to behavior change. They may believe in transactional analysis , classical behaviorism, gestalt therapy or neurolinguistic programming (NLP), and not understand the utility of RET. Rather than attempting to "convert" these individuals, you would do better to show them how RET can be integrated with other approaches. Point out the similarities and differences. Discuss how the language of RET is easily understood and useful in a business environment. Rather than give up their current approach, the potential clients might want to add an RET component that will strengthen their existing program.

Many times individuals are interested in popular "quick fix" approaches which are elegantly marketed and promise amazing results. It is important to point out that RET, while efficient, is not a quick fix approach; rather, what they are buying are results based on years of success around the world. Emphasize that quick fixes are often costly in the long run and do not address the real problems facing organizations today. In order for organizations to meet the challenges of the future, *fundamental changes in beliefs and attitudes need to* take place. RET has a proven method which is efficient without being "psychobabble."

Many managers, when first introduced to RET, conclude that if employees learn to accept themselves as fallible, they will become complacent and quality will suffer. When confronted with this objection, clearly explain that RET emphasizes *doing the best job you can and not giving up quickly.* It keeps people on task when they are feeling anxious and discouraged. RET provides employees with the tools to change their wasteful reactions and then move on to complete the job well. Acceptance of one's fallibility actually *increases* the probability of quality work, because the focus is on long-term satisfaction rather than immediate gratification.

Now let's talk about your first opportunity to sell an RET program to your company or a client. You have studied the basic principles of RET by attending a workshop and read several books so you believe you are prepared. You have incorporated the basic principles into a behaviorally-oriented program and believe the program is much better than before. Now you must convince others.

Preparing Yourself

Before you present your proposal, focus on how you are feeling. Are you somewhat anxious? If so, sit down and find out what you are thinking that might be causing this anxiety. You may discover that you anticipate some resistance. You might also be thinking that you are not adequately prepared to answer all the objections, and that if you fail it would be really unbearable and mean you are inadequate as a salesperson. This kind of thinking will definitely create anxiety!

Now, before you make your presentation, try disputing some of the irrational beliefs that are keeping you anxious.

Your *anticipation* of resistance is not irrational because we know people usually resist new and different ideas and you might not be prepared for all possible objections. However, does the possibility of not doing a successful job the first time mean that you will *never* be successful? Of course not. You might learn from the challenges and be better prepared the *next* time you try to sell the program. If you do not convince the buyer, does this mean you are inadequate as a salesperson? No, it simply means that you need more practice and time to improve. Does everyone succeed the first time when they are learning a new behavior? Of course not. Most people require many trials before they succeed.

Expect to be confronted with resistance, and take it as a challenge, a new learning experience. When you are learning a new sport, it often takes a long time to achieve your goals. Your goals are *long-term,* not immediate. Remind yourself that you will rarely convince everyone all the time. And you don't *have* to be 100 percent successful; you only have to convince a few people. After each failure, sit down and examine your feelings and irrational thoughts, dispute your irrational beliefs and remember that successful sales people are *persistent* and *confident.* They believe in themselves and their product and are willing to persist even when there are no immediate reinforcements. They reinforce *themselves* with their *thoughts.*

CHAPTER 10

Rational Effectiveness Training Programs

STRESS MANAGEMENT: A TWO-DAY PROGRAM

DAY 1

A. Imagery Exercise

- Ask participants to imagine the following event:

As a staff member in the Personnel Department, you arrive at your office on Monday morning to an appointment calendar filled with appointments with colleagues to discuss several important employee relations problems and performance issues.

Your boss enters your office and requests a one-year plan for your department, complete with budget. She adds, "I expect your report before the end of the day today. Cancel all your appointments if you have to because I need this information for tomorrow morning's management team meeting."

You realize that this report will take you more than one day to complete. Although you believe that your boss is generally satisfied with your performance, a somewhat slow work pace has been an issue that she has mentioned in recent performance reviews. "Perhaps you are too perfectionistic" was her comment at your last review.

• Ask participants to write down their feelings and thoughts that occurred during this imagery. Ask them to include *physical* reactions such as tightness in chest or clammy hands.

• Record on a flip chart the different feelings and thoughts offered by the participants.

B. Stress and RET: A Mini-Lecture

Using the above imagery experience, demonstrate the different emotional reactions that individuals have to the same stimulus.

• Connect the different emotional reactions to the different thoughts behind them.

• Discuss the relationship between stress and difficulties in focusing and strong emotional reactions such as anger and fear.

• Provide everyday examples of how stress is compounded by dysfunctional attitudes and emotions.

Introduce the core RET concepts: perfectionism, demandingness, low frustration tolerance, and love slobbism.

Discuss RET's ABC model, integrating examples of stressful experiences offered by the participants. Record these examples on a flip chart in ABC format.

C. Self-Observation

Ask participants to write down incidents and situations in the workplace that cause them stress. Show them how to use the ABC model to format these events, starting with A and C, then filling in the B's, or irrational beliefs.

D. Demonstration of Disputing Techniques

Use participant examples to highlight differences between rational and irrational ideas and demonstrate the disputing process. By learning the different disputing strategies discussed in Chapter 4, participants will have the tools to be able to challenge their irrational thoughts and replace their disturbing ideas with more logical processes.

E. Disputing Techniques: Practice in Triads

Have each participant offer a stressful incident, while the other two members of the triad assist in the disputing process. The objective is for each participant to identify at least two rational statements that can help them reduce their dysfunctional reaction.

F. Questions and Answers

In the large group, ask participants to report their experiences from the previous exercise. Then demonstrate with one or two group members to make sure all participants understand how to uncover irrational beliefs and replace them with rational coping statements.

G. Self-Help Form (see page 99)

Provide each participant with the RET self-help form and reviews its use as a homework assignment to further participants' understanding of the disputing process.

DAY 2

A. Processing the Homework Assignment

Review as many of the group members' completed self-help forms and assist any persons having difficulty in disputing and formulating rational statements.

B. Assertiveness Mini-Lecture

Trainer discusses the following topics:

- changing the activating event
- setting limits for bosses, colleagues, subordinates
- difference between responsible assertiveness and aggression
- risk taking
- negotiating skills

C. " Your Personal Rights" Exercise

Brainstorming with the group their views about personal rights and assertiveness, and records these ideas on a flip chart.

- Ask participants to each select one of the rights that they feel uncomfortable about implementing.

- Ask group members to imagine having this right and consider how it might change their life; their actions; their feelings about themselves and others.

- Ask group members to imagine this right being denied and how their life might change; how their actions might change; and how their feelings about themselves and others might change.

- Ask participants to discuss their reactions in pairs. Have them specify the right they selected, their different feelings and actions, and what they need to work on for the future.

- Have participants write down important rights, along with specific ways to assert these rights.

D. Time Management Skills: A Mini-Lecture

Trainer discusses aspects of time management that produce stress and relates to ABC model.

E. Dear "Doctor Rational" Group Exercise

Provide a basket in the middle of the room. Ask participants to write down the ABCs of a situation that is disturbing to them and address it to "Dear Doctor Rational." Group members then draw a "letter" from the basket and provide an answer (making sure they don't draw their own!) The group then adds other suggestions.

F. Homework Assignments

Provide the following instructions:

• During this week, review your notes on the stressful incident you discussed in the group and repeat several times the rational self-messages that worked for you.

• Then, select two or more *new* stressful experiences. Analyze and dispute each of them on your self-help form, developing rational coping statements that can help you reduce your stress.

SALES EFFECTIVENESS: A ONE-DAY PROGRAM

A. Mini-Lecture on RET

Present the ABC theory of personality, addressing the following:

• The different emotions (functional and dysfunctional) and how they influence thoughts and actions

- How absolutistic thinking undermines people's ability to sell

- The irrational thoughts and beliefs most associated with stress and how they can be disputed

B. Case Example

John is a sales rep who has just been hired by a major health care company which produces and markets both over-the-counter and prescription products. He has completed basic training on the products and is about to begin the work of managing his own territory. Although he will be accompanied by his District Manager for the next two weeks, he is rather anxious about making his initial sales calls to physicians, pharmacists and hospital buyers. Typically, John is bright, energetic, and confident, but he is wavering at this point between guarded enthusiasm and fear of failing at this new job. His first sales call is scheduled for Monday morning.

- Ask participants to put themselves in John's place and offer their responses to the following sentences:

1) I don't remember a thing from basic product training, so_____.

2) What if my district manager sees me as_____? She'll certainly_____.

3) The physician at City Hospital is really tough. I'm sure I will_____.

4) I only have five minutes to explain this new product. I know I'll_____.

5) A poor sales approach on my first time out will mean I'm_____.

- List the group's comments on a flip chart under "Logical" or "Illogical."

Logical	Illogical

• Close with a discussion of anxiety and the self-defeating thoughts and beliefs that perpetuate it.

C. Group Activity: Disputing Self-Defeating Beliefs

• Demonstrate the skills of disputation by challenging the irrational comments and ideas offered by the participants, followed by replacing them with ideas of logical and constructive statements.

• Have participants pair off and practice the disputation method, arguing against their own irrational beliefs as role-played by their partner

D. RET and Increased Productivity: A Mini-Lecture

Discuss the following concepts:

• How to challenge the sources of disturbance

• Conquering need for approval, fear of failure, risk-taking, perfectionistic thinking

• Developing self-tolerance and tolerance for others

• Self-enhancing vs. self-defeating beliefs

• Letting go of self-defeating thoughts and actions

E. Completing an RET Self-Help Form

Ask participants to complete a self-help form on one of their problematic sales situations, including disturbing thoughts, feared events and potential failure-related consequences.

F. Group Exercise in Triads

One at a time, participants share their self-help forms with group members. The two "observer" participants then voice aloud the member's irrational beliefs while he or she practices disputing them.

G. Unlock the Sales Rep in You: Coping Statements

This exercise is designed to help participants create a new form of self-communication to help them remove the barriers noted on their self-help form. With assistance from the group, lead a discussion of techniques for coping with each of the following:

- Turning *fear of failure* into *embracing challenge and opportunity*
- Tolerating weaknesses in yourself to aid in self-acceptance
- Facing difficult situations rather than avoiding them
- Controlling your emotions rather than allowing yourself to be controlled by irrational thoughts

H. Restructured Thinking: Reviewing Participants Coping Statements Individually

Make sure that all participants have now developed useful coping statements for their own problem situations, including ones that will aid them in developing self-direction, acceptance of uncertainty, flexibility, tolerance, and self-acceptance.

Then meet with each participant individually to review their coping statements and methods for using them in their work situations.

Appendix

The following is a sample 6-hour RET stress management program.

Introductory Imagery Exercise *(30 minutes)*

You're working as a staff member in the personnel department. You arrive at your office on Monday morning. Your program for the day is full: you have several appointments with employees about problems they're having and you're sitting in on three performance reviews. Your boss enters your office and says, "Tomorrow morning I need a one-year plan for the Personnel Department with an estimated budget. I need it by the end of the day."

You realize this task will take you more than one day. When you tell your boss your day is already fully committed, he responds, "Cancel all your appointments; this is important. I need the data for tomorrow's meeting of our management team." Without waiting for your response, he leaves your office. Although you know he's generally satisfied with your job performance, he did criticize you in your last review for your slow work-speed, stating that at times, you were "too perfectionistic."

Now open your eyes and write down all the thoughts and

feelings you experienced during this imagery exercise, including physical sensations, such as tightness in the stomach.

Write down on the flip chart the different feelings experienced by participants, and the thoughts that accompanied those feelings. Make the feelings and thoughts as explicit as possible.

Lecture: Stress and RET *(15 minutes)*

• Demonstrate from the previous imagery exercise the *different emotional reactions people can have to the same stimuli.* Be sure to connect the different emotions to the thoughts behind them.

• Discuss the relationship between *strong emotional reactions* such as anger and fear and *stress.* Use examples from participants' daily experiences. Show how typical "A's," such as being busy, explains only a minimal part of the negative stress people experience. Only in very exceptional situations, like physically exhausting work, are stress reactions caused by physical factors. Mainly, stress reactions are exacerbated by people's *attitudes,* especially awfulizing and self- or other-downing.

• Discuss the core issues identified in RET as being causes of stress: perfectionism, demandingness, low frustration tolerance and love slobbism.

• *Introduce the ABC model.* Using real life examples of stressful experiences brought up by the participants, write down these examples in ABC format on a flip chart.

Self-Observation *(15 minutes)*

• Ask trainees to write down concrete incidents and situations in the workplace which cause them stress, in the ABC form. Have them start with A and C, then supply the B's (irrational beliefs) that cause C.

Demonstration of Disputing Techniques *(45 minutes)*

Have two or three group members bring up problems, then use them to demonstrate the disputing process. Stress the differences between *rational* beliefs and *irrational* beliefs, and between *interpretations* and *evaluations*. Demonstrate the different disputing strategies described in Chapter 6. Make sure that problem-presenters wind up with at least two or three rational statements that can be useful to them.

Disputing Exercise in Triads *(15 minutes)*

One at a time, participants bring up an incident that is stressful for them. The other two group members then assist him or her in the disputing process. The end goal for each is to find a rational statement that takes the heat out of the emotional reaction.

Lunch *(1 hour)*

Questions and Answers *(45 minutes)*

Participants report their experiences in subgroups, followed by large-group demonstrations by the trainer. The end goal is for participants to understand the irrationality of their beliefs and to be able to formulate rational coping statements to counter them.

Introduction to the Use of Self-Help Forms (see page 99) *(15 minutes)*

Group Exercise: "Dear Doctor Rational" *(45 minutes)*

Place a basket in the middle of the group. Group mem-

bers write down the ABC's of disturbing situations anony-
mously directed at "Dear Doctor Rational." The leader or a
group member reads one letter at a time; group members discuss the rational alternative.

Homework Assignments *(15 minutes)*

- *Every day this week, reflect on your notes on the stressful
  incident you worked on today. Repeat several times your
  rational self-messages that worked for you.*

- *This week, write down at least two stressful experiences on
  self-help forms. Then dispute your identified irrational
  beliefs and formulate rational coping statements that can
  help you experience less stress. Keep reviewing your forms
  throughout the week.*

OTHER EXERCISES

1) INTRODUCTORY IMAGERY EXERCISE

Objectives: To introduce the ABC model by demonstrating different responses to the same situation; and to begin to
learn the connections between *thoughts* and *feelings*.

Materials: Chalkboard or flip chart, pens, and paper

Procedure: Ask the participants to close their eyes and
imagine the following situation:

*You have prepared a presentation for the Board of
Directors on the results of your research project for your
company. As you are about to begin, you discover a major
statistical error, rendering the data on your transparencies
essentially useless. The President of the Board asks you to*

begin your presentation.

• How do you feel?

• What are your thoughts?

• Open your eyes and write down your thoughts and feelings.

Elicit the different emotional reactions from group members and write them on the board. Explain the difference between *emotions* and *thoughts* and show how certain thoughts will lead to *functional* emotions and behaviors, while others will lead to *disturbed* feelings and behaviors.

2) DIFFICULT DAVID

Objective: To learn the connection between specific irrational beliefs and unproductive emotions and behaviors.

Materials: Transparency of cartoon of "Difficult David" or a flip-chart with beliefs written above his head in balloons; pens and paper

Procedure: Introduce the character "Difficult David" to the group. His beliefs are:

I should feel always happy and relaxed.

I should never make mistakes.

Everybody must like me.

There should be fairness and justice in the world.

Introduce some specific situations that Difficult David may be faced with and ask the group members to write down the feelings and behaviors he's likely to experience given his beliefs.

Example: David's boss criticizes him because he is late for the second time in three weeks.

Pro*bable emotional reactions:* _____

Probable behaviors: _____

David's performance rating is lower than he deserves according to himself and his colleagues.

Probable emotional reactions: _____

Probable behaviors: _____

David is expected to lecture on his specialty: financing exports to southeast Asian countries. The audience consists of financial experts.

Probable emotional reactions: _____

Probable behaviors: _____

Themes for discussion:

- Different beliefs lead to different emotions and behaviors.

- What are David's potential *unproductive* emotions and self-defeating behaviors?

- What might be some potential *rational* beliefs and constructive behaviors?

Variations on this exercise:

- Have one participant take the role of David, voicing aloud his irrational ideas, while the other group members ask disputing questions such as "Where's the evidence...? Could you really not *stand* it?" In this way, training in disputing skills also becomes part of the exercise.

- Choose another cartoon character to illustrate the kinds of situations brought up by the group. In a sales training program, for example, you might present the character of "Sad Sam," who has self-defeating, depressing thoughts over his low sales figures.

3) The TERRIBLE PERSON

Objective: To get insight in the arbitrariness of one's thinking about other people's motives and the emotional and behavioral consequences.

Materials: Paper and pens

Procedure: Tailor your instruction to the trainee. For trainers, for example, this module can be called "The Terrible Trainee." For salespeople, it can be called "The Terrible Customer;" for managers, "The Terrible Subordinate."

Instruction to group members:

Think of an incident with your "terrible (trainee, customer, etc.)" and give a detailed description of his or her horrible and disgusting behavior.

The behavior of this "terrible person" is then presented in detail to the group. Other group members are instructed to think of possible motives for this person's behavior. The person presenting the problem considers the validity of the various suggested motives and then writes down the positive motives he or she considers to be real possibilities. The trainer then asks, "If you could think of this behavior as originating from these positive motives, would it make a difference in how you feel and behave towards this person?"

Group Discussion: How can negative preconceptions and prejudices create difficulties in your interactions with others and interfere with your ability to deal with them?

4) RATIONAL EMOTIVE IMAGERY IN THE GROUP

Objective: To discover rational beliefs and coping statements that can be helpful in managing strong emotions in stressful situations.

Procedure: Choose a common theme: e.g., handling anxiety when speaking to a critical group.

Instruction to group members:

Close your eyes and imagine yourself speaking to a difficult group. You know some of the people. They are experts on the subject of your lecture and you see a lot of critical reactions: some look at you with question marks on their faces, some shake their heads, some whisper to each other, while others have sarcastic smiles. Observe your feelings, and make them stronger—as upset as possible.

Imagine yourself still in the same situation (repeat description). *Now change your strong feelings of upset to milder ones. Keep imagining yourself continuing to talk to this skeptical group, while lowering the intensity of the negative feelings.*

Group discussion:

• What did you do to decrease your upset feeling?

• What did you tell yourself?

• How can you use this imagery practice to learn to change your self-talk and better manage your feelings in real life situations?

Now formulate a specific imagery homework assignment you can practice to prepare yourself for difficult situations.

5) ROLEPLAYING:

A. "DEALING WITH A DIFFICULT CUSTOMER"

Objective: To dispute irrational thoughts causing strong emotions and design a rational way of thinking when confronted with a difficult situation.

Materials: Written role-play instructions

Procedure: Form triads consisting of a hostile customer; Al, the owner of the automotive repair shop; and a coach/observer. Give them the following scenario:

> *The setting is Al's automotive repair shop. A hostile customer bursts into the office demanding to see the owner. The customer's face is beet red, he looks as if he's about to split a gut, and he's muttering profanities. He says, "This is the fourth day this week I've brought my car in; and not only is the original problem not corrected, but now it's leaking transmission fluid and the brakes don't work at all. I'll be damned if I'm paying you another dime, and I put a stop payment on the other checks I gave you this week. I've also contacted my lawyer, and you'll be hearing from her. So give me my key back right now or I'll call the police."*

Background information: This customer has been coming to Al's for two years. There are three cars in his family, all of which get serviced at Al's. This week, Al hired two new mechanics, and it's possible they did screw up. However, Al had personally approved the order for the new parts, and will therefore have to eat the cost of any mistakes.

During the role-play: The person playing "Al" is to resolve the problem with the customer, disputing any beliefs he has that might lead to rage, hostility, and a counterproductive response.

After the role-play: The coach in the triad asks the person playing Al what s/he was feeling, and what was the event that led to these feelings. What were "Al's" beliefs about these events that actually caused the feelings? The coach then helps "Al" dispute any unproductive beliefs and assists him to formulate productive rational coping statements. The coach then asks "Al" if s/he responded appropriately, and if the problem has been resolved.

Themes for group discussion:

• Discuss the relationship between rational thinking and controlling your own behavior when under attack.

• What are the short-term and long-term advantages of controlling anger in relations with customers?

• Discuss the differences between *assertive* behavior and *aggressive* behavior.

Variations:

• Replay the situation. This time, "Al" is instructed to use the rational coping statements while playing the role. Group members then give feedback to Al on the difference between Al's first and second role-plays.

• Replay the situation, without switching roles. This time, the "customer" is to use disputing techniques to control his/her anger.

B) HANDLING CRITICISM

Procedure: Form triads consisting of a product manager, a vice president, and a co-worker/coach. Give them the following scenario:

You are in the product manager's office. The product manager has recently completed a proposal for a new line of appliances. She discussed the idea with the vice president a few weeks ago. The VP loved the idea, and asked her to write up a formal proposal. The product manager put tremendous time and energy into completing the proposal, and believed she had done a first-class job. This morning, however, the VP personally returned the proposal to her, stating that it was a lousy idea and it would just be laughed at if it was brought to the Board.

Background information: The product manager has been feeling stymied in her current position for some time. She is also due to be considered for a promotion. This proposal, if accepted, could have been the ticket to that promotion.

After the VP leaves the product manager's office, the product manager now stews aloud over the rejection, while the co-worker/coach listens attentively. She makes the following self-sabotaging statements: "I'll never get anywhere in this company;" "The vice president hates all my ideas; so why did I even bother?" "This company is the pits; they never want to be innovative around here;" "I'm never going to give any of my good ideas again."

The coach now helps the product manager to dispute her self-defeating thoughts, and replace them with more productive, creative thoughts.

Discussion themes:

• What is the relationship between being creative and being able to handle negative criticism?

• How can developing high frustration tolerance and perseverance help you promote your career in the long run?

C) Handling a Negative Image

Form triads and ask them to role-play the following situation:

An employee is suddenly fired by the manager. Three employees who are colleagues and friends of the fired employee refuse to work the next day. They feel betrayed and tell the manager they feel they can no longer trust him.

The manager is to dispute any potential irrational beliefs, such as "My employees *must* like me in order for me to motivate them to work."

Discussion themes:

• How does love-slobbism hinder people performing their role as managers?

• What are the differences between being *liked* and being *respected* as a leader?

D) Handling Risk

You are the publisher of a group of profitable small community papers. You are presented with the opportunity to purchase a small business weekly. It has an excellent advertising base, but the current publishers run out of capital. You are suspicious of your talents as a publisher. You wish you could scientifically determine the success or failure of a publication. Discuss with the group you're working with all the fears you have about this enterprise. The group rationally disputes all your fears. Then based on these rational disputes, make a decision as to whether or not to take the risk.

Discussion Themes

• What is the relationship between risk-taking and being successful?

• What is the relationship between risk-taking and creativity?

6) WRITTEN EXERCISE

Objective: To learn how to analyze problems by writing them down in the ABC format.

Materials: Self-help forms (see page 99)

Procedure: Describe a disturbing work situation most participants can relate to, such as time management. Example:

You have just returned from vacation. There are 15 tele-

phone messages, your in-basket is piled a foot high, and your assistant hasn't culled urgent items from it. One of your subordinates is waiting at your door to discuss an important personal matter; some of the equipment in the plant has worn out and a crew is waiting for your response on whether to repair or replace it; and the vice president has called an important meeting to start in a half hour (which you suspect will last most of the day). You desperately need a cup of coffee, but you can't afford the time it will take.

Your thoughts: "I feel like taking the plane back to Aruba. How can I possibly deal with this mess? I'll get ulcers sitting in that meeting all day, knowing everything else that's being neglected. This must be some kind of conspiracy against me. Surely no else comes back from vacation to this. It's just not fair." Now write down this problem situation on your self-help form, identifying the ABC's. Dispute any ideas that are irrational, then replace them with more rational thoughts. Then come up with an action plan for taking care of your workload.

Group discussion:

Go through the ABCDE sequence step-by-step with the group. Identify the dysfunctional C's (feelings) and the irrational thoughts underlying them. Teach participants the importance of doing *emotional* self-management before they embark on solving the *practical* problems.

After group members have worked on their self-help forms on their own, discuss the responses in the large group.

7) DEBATE ON NATIONAL TELEVISION

Objective: To learn to discriminate between rational and irrational beliefs and to learn disputing skills.

Materials: Two pieces of cardboard, labeled "Party for the Advancement of Irrational Beliefs (PAIB)" and "Party for Rational Beliefs (PRB)" and 3 tables

Procedure: Choose two representatives of the "PAIB," two representatives of the "PRB," and a chairperson. The representatives are to sit at separate tables with the PAIB and PRB signs. The chairperson is seated at the middle table. The representatives of the Party for Rational Beliefs are now to debate issues and incidents with the representative of the Party for the Advancement of Irrational Beliefs presented to them by the chairperson. E.g.: "What do you think of redesigning all product packaging during the next year?" The debaters advance their views and try to convince the other team. The other group members can pose questions and problems to the debaters by writing them down on slips of paper and giving them to the chair, who passes them to the debaters.

8) DEAR DOCTOR RATIONAL

Objective: To learn disputing skills and rational problem-solving.

Materials: Basket, paper and pens

Procedure: Group members write anonymous letters to "Dear Doctor Rational" and place them in the basket. The leader or group members read the letters, with group members taking turns in playing the role of Dr. Rational, who responds by giving rational ways of thinking and rational solutions.

9) RISK-TAKING

Objective: To learn how to experiment with taking risks

and to learn how to dispute the ideas that block risk-taking.

Procedure: Give the group the following instruction:

Do something in the group during the day that you consider risky behavior—something that normally generates strong negative emotions like shame or fear that would keep you from doing the behavior in real life. You could improvise a speech, ask someone to tell you what his/her income is, sing a children's song, or tell the group your most embarrassing situation. Be sure you're not physically hurting somebody else or yourself and don't do something that's against the law. Now write down your planned risk-taking situation in ABC format, and dispute any irrational beliefs that might interfere with your actually performing the risky behavior.

Discussion themes:

• How did you handle your feelings of shame or fear?

• What are the advantages of risk-taking in daily life—in the workplace, social relations, etc.?

• What assignments can you give yourself in daily life to reduce your emotional blocks to doing new or difficult things?

10) WRITING LETTERS TO YOUR IRRATIONAL SELF

Objective: To advance transfer of learning to the real-life situation at the end of the training.

Materials: Paper, pens, envelopes, stamps

Procedure: Give the following instructions to the group:

"Imagine yourself 10 years from now—a much wiser and more rational person. Now write a letter to your current self

about your current problems and irrational beliefs, contain-
ing advice on what you can do to overcome your emotional
disturbance and problematic behavior. Mail this letter to
yourself on the last day of the workshop."

11) EXAGGERATING DISASTERS

Objective: To learn disputing by humor and exaggeration.

Materials: Paper and pencils.

Procedure: Ask group members to write down a specific anticipated crisis and the worst thing that might happen to them in that situation. Examples: "My boss fires me; I lose my voice during a public speech; My wife divorces me;" etc. One at a time, group members read their situation aloud. The other group members then exaggerate the disaster even further by thinking up more possible catastrophic outcomes.

Discussion themes:

• How can use of humor and exaggeration be helpful in the disputing process?

• What happens when you assess the actual probability of the worst happening?

• What are the advantages of developing worst-case scenarios?

12) READ IT ON THE FRONT PAGE

Objective: To learn disputing by humor and exaggeration.

Procedure: Give the following instructions to the group: "Imagine looking at the front page of the newspaper and seeing your terrible mistakes and disasters in headlines on the front page. The front page is covered with pictures and special reports about you and your disastrous mistakes, including shocked comments by some of your closest friends and colleagues.

Discussion themes:

• [See exercise 11.]

• How does exaggerating your own importance in other people's perception interfere with your effectiveness?

13) YOU ARE THE PERFECT PERSON

Objective: To learn to dispute irrational perfectionistic demands on oneself.

Materials: Paper and pencils

Procedure: Instruct the group to:

Write a one-page essay about yourself as a Perfect Person, who never makes mistakes or has any weaknesses. Present this ideal person to the group. Give a description in 15 lines.

Discussion themes:

• What are the advantages and disadvantages of being imperfect?

• Discuss the relationship between perfectionism and feeling insecure.

• What kinds of questions can you ask yourself to dispute your irrational demands for perfection?

14) CAN YOU LIVE WITH YOUR BAD TRAITS?

Objective: To learn self-acceptance.

Materials: Paper and pencils

Procedure: Give each group member 10 pieces of paper. On the left side of each paper, participants are to write down one *good* trait they have. On the right side, they are to write down one *bad* trait. When they have done this with all 10 sheets, instruct them to tear the papers down the middle and throw away the left sides (the good traits). Then ask them to read their ten bad traits and consider if it is possible to accept themselves if they had only these traits. What opportunities would they still have in life with these traits?

Discussion themes:

• What are the advantages of having bad traits?

• If you accept yourself with your bad traits, will it stop you from improving yourself?

15) YOUR PERSONAL RIGHTS

Objective: To identify ideas that interfere with assertiveness and to practice in imagery changing these ideas and acting more assertively.

Materials: Chalk board or flip chart

Procedure: Start by asking group members what are their personal rights, and write them on the board.

Then have them enumerate the risks in exercising these rights. "How can you determine what to do when your rights conflict with those of others?" Next, ask group members to select one of the rights they feel *uncomfortable* accepting for themselves, and to imagine themselves having this right. "How would your life change? How would you act? How would you feel about yourself and other people?"

• Next, imagine yourself *without* this right. "How would your life change? How would you act? How would you feel about yourself? Other people? How would your life change?"

• Last, divide into pairs and discuss the right you selected. How did you *feel* accepting this right? In what ways did you *act* differently? What are you going to do in the future?

16) THE HOT SEAT

Objective: To learn how to manage your thoughts and emotions when criticized.

Materials: One chair placed in the middle of the group

Procedure: Ask for a volunteer to sit in the "hot seat." Instruct other group members to give the volunteer feedback on his or her behavior in the group by offering one positive statement and one negative statement. The group leader coaches the person in the hot seat to handle the feedback by helping him/her construct rational coping statements to keep himself or herself calm.

Discussion themes:

• How can you make *constructive* use of negative feedback in your daily life?

• How can you react better behaviorally when you receive negative feedback in your daily life?

17) THE RATIONAL AND IRRATIONAL CHAIR

Objective: To learn to dispute irrational ideas.

Materials: One chair with a cardboard sign "IRRA-TIONAL CHAIR" and another one with a cardboard "RATIONAL CHAIR"

Procedure: Place the two chairs in the middle of the room. Participants bring in an ABC analysis of a disturbing situation. One participant is invited to sit in the "irrational chair" and formulate irrational statements. Another person sits down in the "rational chair" and offers rational counterarguments. Other participants can jump in the "rational chair" as an alter ego. The group leader directs the exercise by asking participants to change chairs when irrational arguments are used in the "rational chair" and vice versa.

Discussion themes:

• Some useful ways you can train yourself in daily life to improve your internal dialogue when confronted with difficult situations include writing a diary, role-playing situations with a colleague, and using the "two-chair" technique.

RET ATTITUDE PREPARATION

SELF-HELP FORM

Rational Effectiveness Training Systems
45 East 65th Street, New York, N.Y. 10021
(212) 535-0822

(A) ACTIVATING EVENTS:. Common situations that I get frustrated and upset about_____

_____

(C) CONSEQUENCES: Frustrating reactions or self-defeating behavior that I produced and would like to change_____

_____

(B) BELIEFS:-Irrational Beliefs (IBs) leading to my CONSEQUENCE (emotional disturbance or self-defeating behavior). Circle all that apply to these ACTIVATING EVENTS (A). ↓	**(D) DISPUTES** for each circled IRRATIONAL BELIEF. Examples: *"Why* MUST I do very well?" *"Where is it written* that I am a BAD PERSON?" *"Where is the evidence* that I MUST be approved or accepted?"	**(E) EFFECTIVE RATIONAL BELIEFS** (RBs) to replace my IRRATIONAL BELIEFS (IBs). Examples: *"I'd* PREFER *to do very well but I don't* HAVE *to." "I am a PERSON WHO acted badly, not a BAD PERSON." "There is no evidence that* I HAVE *to be approved, though I would* LIKE *to be."*
1. I MUST do well or very well!		
2. I am a BAD OR WORTHLESS PERSON when I act weakly or stupidly.		

3. I MUST be approved or accepted by people I find important!

4. People MUST treat me fairly and give me what I NEED!

5. People MUST live up to my expectations or it is TERRIBLE!

6. I CAN'T STAND really bad things or very difficult people!

7. My work MUST have few major hassles or troubles.

8. It's AWFUL or
HORRIBLE when major
things don't go my way!

9. I CAN'T STAND IT
when work is really
unfair!

10. I NEED a good deal of
immediate gratification
and HAVE to feel
miserable when I
don't get it!

Additional Irrational Beliefs:

(F) **FEELINGS** and **BEHAVIORS** I experienced after arriving at my **EFFECTIVE RATIONAL BELIEFS**_____

_____

_____

_____

References

Beck, A. T. (1976). *Cognitive therapy and the emotional disorders*. New York: International Universities Press.

Bordin, E. S. (1979). The generalizability of the psychoanalytic concept of the working alliance. *Psychotherapy: Theory, Research and Practice, 16,* 252-260.

Dryden, W. (1985). Foreword to A. Ellis, *Overcoming resistance: Rational-emotive therapy with difficult clients.* New York: Springer.

Ellis, A. (1958). Rational psychotherapy. *Journal of General Psychology, 59,* 35-49.

Ellis, A. (1962). *Reason and emotion in psychotherapy.* New York: Lyle Stuart.

Ellis, A. (1972). *Executive leadership: A rational approach.* New York: Institute for Rational-Emotive Therapy.

Ellis, A. (1985). *Overcoming resistance: Rational-emotive therapy with difficult clients.* New York: Springer.

Ellis, A. & Harper, R. A. (1975). *A new guide to rational living.* North Hollywood, CA: Wilshire Books.

IJzermans, T. G. & Dirkx, C. (1992). *Beren op de weg, spinself in je hoofd. Omgaan met emoties op het werk: De rationele effectiviteitraining.* Zaltbommel, The Netherlands: Thema.

Lange, A. (1987). *Strategieën in directive therapie.* Deventer, The Netherlands : Van Loghum Slaterus.

Lange, A. J. & Jakubowski, P. (1976). *Responsible assertive behavior: Cognitive/behavioral procedures for trainers.* Champaign, IL: Research Press.

Lazarus, A. (1976). *Multi-modal behavior therapy.* New York: Springer.

Lazarus, R. S. & Folkman, S. (1984). *Stress, appraisal, and coping.* New York: Springer.

Mahoney, M. (1974). *Cognition and behavior modification.* Cambridge, MA: Ballinger.

Maultsby, M. (1975). *Help yourself to happiness.* New York: Institute for Rational-Emotive Therapy.

Meichenbaum, D. (1977). *Cognitive-behavior modification: An integrative approach.* New York: Plenum.

Molen, H. T., van der. (1984). *Aan verlegenheid valt iets to doen: een cursus in plaats van therapie.* Deventer, The Netherlands: Van Loghum Slaterus.

Oomkes, F. R. (1992). *Training als beroep: Sociale en intercul-turele vaardigheid. Deel 1: Trainingstheorie. Deel 2: Oefeningen in sociale vaardigheid.* Amsterdam, The Netherlands: Boom.

Rabkin, R. (1977). *Strategic psychotherapy. Brief and sympto-matic treatment.* New York: Basic Books.

Schouten, J. (1977). *Ik ben d'r ook nog.* Amsterdam, The Netherlands: Boom.

Son, M. van. (1978). *Sociale vaardigheidstherapie.* Amsterdam, The Netherlands: Swets en Zeitlinger.

Spivack, G., Platt, J., and Shure, M. (1976). *The problem-solving approach to adjustment.* San Francisco, CA: Jossey Bass.

Additional Readings and Audiotapes:

Baldon, A. & Ellis, A. (1993). *RET problem solving workbook.* New York: Institute for Rational-Emotive Therapy

Bernard, M. E. (1991). *Using rational-emotive therapy effectively: A practitioner's guide.* New York: Plenum.

Dryden, W. and Gordon, J. (1993). *Peak performance.* London, England: Mercury Business Books.

Ellis, A. (1988). *How to stubbornly refuse to make yourself miserable about anything—yes anything!* Secaucus, NJ: Carol Publishing.

Ellis, A. (1996). *Better, deeper and more enduring brief therapy.* New York: Brunner/Mazel.

Ellis, A. and Knaus, W. J. (1977). *Overcoming procrastination.* New York: Penguin.

Ellis, A. & Lange, A. (1994). *How to keep people from pushing your buttons.* Secaucus, NJ: Carol Publishing Group.

Mind over myths (Audiotape). (1987). New York: Institute for Rational-Emotive Therapy.

Robin, M. & Balter, R. (1995). *Performance anxiety.* Holbrook, MA: Adams.

Walen, S., DiGiuseppe, R. & Dryden, W. (1992). *A practitioner's guide to rational-emotive therapy.* New York: Oxford University Press.